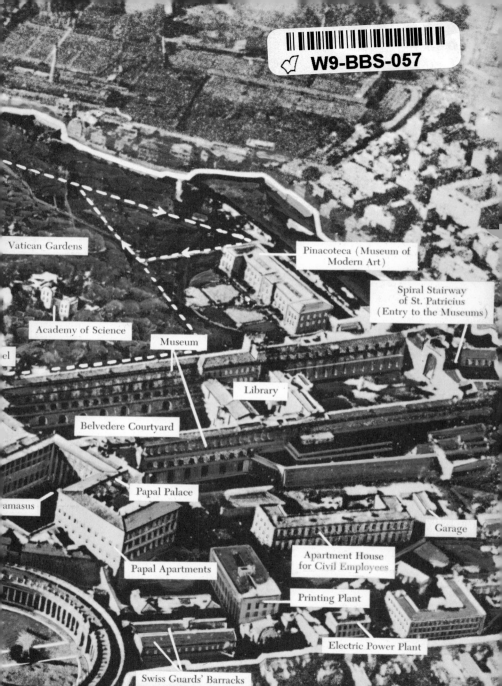

Vatican Gardens

Pinacoteca (Museum of Modern Art)

Spiral Stairway of St. Patricius (Entry to the Museums)

Academy of Science

Museum

Library

Belvedere Courtyard

Papal Palace

Garage

amasus

Apartment House for Civil Employees

Papal Apartments

Printing Plant

Electric Power Plant

Swiss Guards' Barracks

Nero's
g site of
St. Peter

The
VATICAN

The
VATICAN

Its Organization, Customs,
and Way of Life

by JEAN NEUVECELLE

Translated from the French by
GEORGE LIBAIRE

CRITERION BOOKS   NEW YORK

Contents

Illustrations

Part One

THE POPE

I

The Smallest State in the World

THERE IS THE IRON CUR-
tain; and there is also the Bronze Door. At that doorway
stand the Swiss of the Papal Guard, armed with halberds,
and it gives access to the smallest State in the world,
where rules an old man clad all in white. His State, a mere

3

precinct in the shadow of a cathedral, is no more extensive than a single ward of a city like New York. It is
built upon a cemetery. If you but scratch the soil, you will
come upon deep catacombs—the underground passages
where first the pagans and afterwards the earliest Christians laid their dead. And long ago, beneath the very
ground where the pontifical State now stands, there was a
circus where the disciples of the new religion were
martyred by Nero. There, head downward, the first in
line of the rulers of this State was crucified.

Admission to Vatican City may be gained by way of
three main frontier posts: the Bronze Door, the Gate of
the Bells, and St. Anna's Gate. There are no customs
officials at the border but there is a double barrier to
pass. First there are the Swiss, who will present halberds
if you are a bishop or if you have the mien of an ambas-
sador. Next come the pontifical gendarmes, who will direct
you to the bureau of admissions. There you surrender
your identification card and state whom you propose to
call upon. Following a check by telephone, you will be
handed a document—and likewise a prescribed itinerary.
Moreover, the pontifical gendarmes are posted in such a
way as not to allow the pedestrian (for such the visitor
almost invariably is) out of their sight during the whole
course of his route.

The full circuit of Vatican City, which Rome encom-
passes on every side, requires, on foot, three-quarters of
an hour. To skirt the ancient walls makes a charming
walk, and one which is favored by young lovers. The
Papal State is ringed about by a circle of courting couples.
As a matter of fact, though, it is not always possible to
distinguish the precise boundaries of the City; for it has,
in proportion to its size, the greatest number of extra-
territorial possessions of any State. The outlying terri-

tories over which the Pope holds full temporal sway are more extensive than is Vatican City itself. Almost all are situated within Rome or in the immediate neighborhood of the Eternal City. On the other hand, Vatican City loses its citizens as soon as they no longer reside within its boundaries. The only exceptions are cardinals and nuncios, who retain their Vatican citizenship even though they dwell outside.

The Apostolic Palace, which is the Vatican proper, comprises approximately 10,000 halls, passages, suites, rooms, and storage rooms. The windows total 12,523; and there are 997 flights of stairs, of which thirty are secret and fifteen are spiral stairways. In addition to the apartments of state and the Pope's private apartment, an indefinite number of lodgings nestle within the walls, on the roofs, in the turrets, and down in the cellars of this jumble of buildings, the construction of which, begun six centuries ago, is still in progress. Cardinals, monks, nuns, and the families of secular employees reside there.

Another considerable portion of the territory is taken up by the Basilica of St. Peter, the largest church in the world. Many are the visitors who find it too shiny and ornate. The concept of a sanctuary, for them, is associated with the idea of Gothic cathedrals and the mysterious half-dark. Be that as it may, St. Peter's is extraordinarily harmonious and has great beauty of line. It is 651 feet long and 435 feet high. The Confession baldachin, surmounting the high altar, is as tall as the Louvre. Within one of the four central pillars, the graceful Church of San Carlino, at Rome, could be entirely enclosed. St. Peter's contains 777 columns, 44 altars, and 395 statues—

which last are of no mean proportions. The miter alone
of St. Augustine is appreciably taller than the average
height of a grown man; whereas the famous statue of
St. Peter, with its bronze foot worn smooth by pilgrims'
kisses, is life-size.

The maintenance of St. Peter's is administered by a
"corporation" which has been in existence since the sixteenth century with its membership descending, as a
rule, from father to son. They are called the San Pietrini.
Numbering about seventy, they have a special uniform, and they undergo a long course of training which
starts in childhood; for their main activity is displayed
not only within the church but to an even greater extent
upon the exterior, on the dome. They are veritable acro-
bats, with a technique all their own—a trade secret—for
climbing to the tops of the columns when the church is
to be decorated for festive occasions; and for walking
about, their feet higher than their heads, over the interior
surfaces of the dome in order to close a window or dust
the golden lettering, every character of which is as tall
as a man. For such tasks as these they use ropes, which
they make fast to the capital of a column or to some
marble angel.

But the exploit for which they have deserved world
renown is the illumination of the façade of the basilica.
A month's time is needed to prepare for this, since it
requires the setting-out of five thousand lamps and a
thousand torchlights. To fill the torches, which are huge
metal dishes, some thirty-five hundred pounds of fat are
melted down. Several miles of heavy rope are needed to
enable the San Pietrini to clamber along the full width of
the façade and over the dome, and up the lantern and
the great globe and cross which surmount the church.
Occasionally, looped fast to their ropes, the San Pietrini

swing out into space, the better to reach some point where a lamp is called for.

The illumination itself takes place in two stages. An hour after the Angelus the lamps are lighted, delicately outlining the elevations and contours of the façade and dome. Then comes the turn of the cross atop the basilica. The chief of the San Pietrini swarms up it in person at the head of his whole troupe; and thus he gives the signal for a frantic dance of tiny black figures, barely perceptible against the gathering twilight. In a matter of minutes they have set all the torches flaring at once, and the façade and the dome awaken to quivering life as a glowing sheet of flame, streaming up the pilasters and writhing along the ridges and peaks, shadows forth the great marble statues that adorn the pediment. . . . Of late years, however, for reasons of economy and safety, the illumination has been done with electric light. The mere cost of the insurance premiums on the San Pietrini had become, as a matter of fact, prohibitive.

Vatican City numbers among its possessions thirty squares and streets, fifty outlying properties, two churches (besides St. Peter's), a parish, and a mountain, topped by the antennæ of Radio Station HVJ; a railroad station, four post offices, a court of law, two jails, four newspapers or periodicals (the official bulletin *Acta Apostolicæ Sedis*, in Latin, and the unofficial daily, *L'Osservatore Romano*, in Italian, as are also *L'Osservatore della Domenica*, a weekly, and *Ecclesia*, a monthly), and four military barracks. The population totals 1,031, of whom 750 are men and 281 women, comprising 153 households, with 57 children. The inhabitants are drawn from fifteen nationalities. Italian is the official language of Vatican City, whereas that of the Holy See is Latin. The official religion is Catholicism, the national colors are white and yellow, and the national anthem is a composition of Gounod's. Automobiles bear a special license plate marked SCV. The Vatican military outnumber the civilians; and the majority of civilians are clergy.

Vatican City is not the Holy See: this latter designation signifies the government of the Church. The Church can exist without any temporal sovereignty whatsoever. That was the condition obtaining throughout the first seven centuries of the Christian era and again from 1870 to 1929, at which date the Popes renounced once and for all their claim to Rome and set up a temporal State in Vatican City. Actions initiated by the Holy See do not necessarily involve Vatican City, and vice versa. For example, Vatican City is a member of certain international organizations, such as the World Postal Union. The Pope is both the leader of Catholic Christendom and, since 1929, sovereign ruler of Vatican City, but this designation holds only sixth place among his titles, following after that of Bishop of Rome, Patriarch of the West, and so forth.

The principle of the separation of Church and State is admitted at Vatican City, after a fashion. State government is assured by means of the agencies to which the Pope has delegated his powers. At all events, Vatican City, existing only as a function of the Holy See, serves to provide it with a body—the bare minimum of territory sufficient to symbolize its sovereign independence. Vatican City can have, then, no political life of its own, nor any autonomous development; and no revolution can possibly take place there. Its existence depends entirely upon the volition of the Pope. Not only is the Pope a sovereign, vested with the triple powers of legislature, executive, and judiciary: he is proprietor of the entire State as well—but he delegates the greater portion of his temporal powers to a Cardinals' Commission.

Two cardinals, Canali and Pizzardo, serve on the Commission. The other members are Prince Carlo Pacelli, the Pope's nephew, and Count Pietro Enrico Galeazzi. Among them they exercise the power of the executive, and they control the life of the City down to the most minute detail. Every financial, economic, administrative, fiscal, and military problem is screened by the Cardinals' Commission. Nothing escapes them, whether it be the birth of a child in the home of one of the pastry cooks or the placing under arrest of a pontifical gendarme who has gone over the hill or the installation of a new antenna at the radio station. Cardinal Canali, a most important functionary of the Curia (Grand Penitentiary, Grand Master of the Order of the Holy Sepulchre, etcetera), is also a lynx-eyed administrator, and it is not unheard of for him to concern himself directly with the regulations governing the manner of distribution, through the State commissaries, of the rations of bread, sugar, vegetables, oil, and wine.

Next after him, the man who holds the highest post in the unofficial hierarchy of Vatican City is a layman, Count Galeazzi, architect-in-charge of the "Reverend Fabric of St. Peter." He is a great administrator and an intimate of the Sovereign Pontiff. He is half-brother to the Pope's personal physician who, surprising though it may seem, is an oculist by profession.

One day, as Cardinal Pacelli, who had not yet become Pius XII, was passing along the Via Sistina, at Rome, he beheld an enormous eye gazing at him from atop an office building. It was the advertising sign of Professor Galeazzi,

a celebrated oculist. The future Pope, who needed his
eyeglasses changed, went up to the Professor's office; and
he became his faithful client. This was but a short while
before he received the tiara. On the day of the Conclave,
as he was returning from the Sistine Chapel after the final
balloting, Cardinal Pacelli fell and hurt his arm. He refused attention, however; and within a few hours he had
become Supreme Head of the Church. Not until the end
of that emotion-packed day did he think of his injury;
and then, since Professor Galeazzi was the only doctor
with whom he was personally acquainted, he sent for
him. From then on, whenever the Pope was ill, the oculist
was summoned. Not many months after Pius XII's accession, Professor Galeazzi received the title of Chief Physician to the Pontiff.

As for his brother, the Count already was the Vatican
City architect. His position and duties are such as to
bring him into frequent contact with the Sovereign Pontiff; a circumstance which vests him with great authority.
His advice is heeded, his orders are obeyed, his recom-
mendations are sought after. Count Galeazzi is eager to
keep abreast of the times. He has traveled widely, visiting
the United States in particular on a number of occasions.
From those visits began his friendship with the man who
was destined afterward to become Cardinal Spellman.

The fortunate citizens who are under the administration of Vatican City pay no taxes. They do not even have
to pay rent, since the whole reason for their "living in"
is that their duties are such as to require it of them. They
are exempt from military service. The State, at greatly
reduced prices, furnishes them with bread, milk, sugar,

and cloth from official stores, which are the only shops allowed; and their medicines they procure from the State Pharmacy, which is run by the Brotherhood of St. John the Divine. Their dogs pay no tax, either. Theoretically, duties are assessed upon products coming from abroad and there is a set scale of charges. Such transactions, however, are subject to private arrangement between the citizens and the government.

The City draws its revenues from the sale of postage stamps (28 series since 1929). This brings in about two million lire a month, but there is no way of determining the amounts paid by collectors for rare items. The State realizes a small profit, too, from the retailing of American cigarettes at a slight surcharge, and from alcoholic beverages. Obviously, when one considers the functionaries, the army, and public works, all this revenue together is not nearly enough to defray expenses. It follows, then, that Vatican City operates at a deficit. But no such thing as a regular budget is ever brought in, nor is there ever any advance estimate of expenses. When the bills are presented, the Holy See makes up the difference. The Temporal State is a subhead in the Vatican's bookkeeping.

Among the more visible attributes of Vatican sovereignty is its railroad station. Now and then it does receive a load of freight. But the station is there primarily as proof of the State's independence, and it is for that reason that it has an imposing platform and a few yards of track which join it up to the Italian railway system. There is an actual iron curtain which can be closed, thus cutting off all communication between that system and the Vatican siding. There *is* no railway personnel but there is a sta-

tion master. He has the title of *cavalière* but no cap or
uniform. The Pope has no train, no ships, no airplane.
But there is a huge fleet of motor trucks and personal
vehicles. Several of the passenger automobiles have been
specially constructed for the Sovereign Pontiff, with a
throne installed in place of the usual rear seat. When the
Pope goes "abroad," however, he prefers to use a standard
model.

Three law courts serve to dispense justice to the citizens
of Vatican City: the District Court, which is housed
within the City itself, and the Court of Appeals and the
Supreme Tribunal, which have their chambers in Rome,
in the extraterritorial palaces. Cases at law are extremely
rare, primarily because the citizens are law-abiding but
also because the authorities prefer to turn offenders over
to the secular arm of Italian justice. Deliberations concerning offenses against ecclesiastical laws of course fall
within the competence of Church tribunals—which must
by no means be confused with the temporal jurisdiction
of Vatican City. There are two City jails, both of which
are furnished with comfortable cells having all the con-
veniences of modern hygiene; but they rarely have an
occupant. During the last war, the prisons were used to
store foodstuffs.

A calm like that of the Sabbath broods over the streets
and peaceful squares of Vatican City. The military are
out in force. Their bearing is jaunty and their uniforms

range in style all the way from the Renaissance down to
the period of Napoleon III. Walking along beside the wall
of an extensive building with closed windows is an aged
ecclesiastic. He is a cardinal, the curator of the greatest
library in the world. Other passers-by are a councilor of
the Japanese Embassy, Count Della Torre, publisher of
the *Osservatore Romano,* the Pope's nephew, the Pope's
barber.

Everybody in the square knows everybody else and
greets him ceremoniously. An outsider is instantly recog-
nizable as such. Perfect decorum is the rule in every
street. Not to mention morality.

There are no cafés, no restaurants, no newspaper kiosks;
all commercial enterprise is forbidden by law. The bar of
St. Peter's sacristy, patronized by canons and gendarmes,
closes at noon. One last resort remains for the thirsty, the
canteen of the Swiss Guards. But you have to show your
credentials.

Industrial life and the arts and crafts are limited in
scope. Nevertheless, there is an entire section of the City
which resounds with the roar of motors and machinery.
There is a famous studio at the Vatican which produces
mosaics; and the uniforms for the army are made within
the walls. Also, there are two great printing plants one of
which, the Polyglot Press, has fonts of type of every
language in the world. The workers in that plant are
monks bound to absolute secrecy and never, for as long
as Church history runs, has there been a defection from
the order.

Functionaries of the State administration, employees
and laborers, are poorly paid. Low wages are compen-
sated for, however, by gifts of rations, by the installation
of a canteen, and by the positive assurance of being able

to live out one's days in the shadow of the cathedral with
no risk of losing one's job—and secure, above all, from
the storms of all sorts of revolution by which other States
are overturned. Vatican officials prudently hold out a little
each month from the pay envelopes of their functionaries
to provide for their burial. On the other hand, every time
a Pope dies, a gratuity is paid to all those who have tasks
to perform on account of the election of his successor.
For this reason it is that whenever times are hard, employees of the Vatican may be heard to exclaim: *"Ah, se
solo potesse morire il papa!"* ("Oh, if only the Pope would
die!")

There is no such thing as a labor union at the Vatican.
Some trifling gestures toward the founding of one were
manifested at the time of the Liberation, when the
streets of Rome were overrun with truckloads of young
men wearing astrakhan caps and waving red flags and
singing the *Internationale* in Italian. But, after discreetly
deporting the hotheads, the patriarchal administration
soon regained the upper hand.

In the administration of Vatican City the firemen constitute an élite corps, and well do they merit the proud
name. They are housed in one of the most beautiful of
the Vatican courtyards, the Belvedere, and are outfitted
with jeeps and all the most up-to-date apparatus of a
model fire department. Twice daily, patrols go through
the immense Vatican Palace from top to bottom, furnished with an enormous bunch of keys which admit
them to every nook and cranny. And, as proof of how
highly the firemen are regarded at the Vatican, it is their
prerogative, when they too are well along in years, to
keep the pontifical elevators running. The Palace of the
Vatican has several lifts. The oldest connects the public

audience chambers with the Pope's private apartment, which is on the floor above. That one is reserved for the sole use of the Sovereign Pontiff. It was installed in 1850, and at the outset it was operated by machinery powered by the arms of a pair of brawny footmen. The last time that system was used was in 1903, to allow King Edward VII of England to call upon Leo XIII. In the pontificate of Pius XI the cage of the lift was furnished with a silver medallion bearing the image of St. Christopher, protector of travelers.

II

Morning at the Palace

THE SOVEREIGN PONTIFF
has just finished dressing. On the third floor of the
Vatican Palace, the only lighted windows are those of his
private apartment. The great clock of St. Peter's has not
yet struck seven. It is a cold day. The vast empty square
and the Bernini colonnade are shrouded in fog.

The Pope has come out of the bathroom where, each in
its carefully appointed place, are lined up his electric
razor, his toilet articles, and the chest weights with which
he exercised until his late illness. He is wearing a plain
white cassock. Absorbed in prayer, he paces back and
forth in his bedroom, which is furnished with a burled-
walnut bedstead, an easy chair, a *prie-dieu*, and a table
piled high with documents. There is absolute silence,
broken only at regular intervals by the measured tread of
a pontifical gendarme. A goldfinch and two canaries are
fluttering about the room, occasionally perching on his
shoulder and venturing a shrill chirp. These little birds
provide his first company of the day. The goldfinch,
named Gretel by Mother Pasqualina (the Bavarian nun
who tidies up the Holy Father's simple quarters), loves
the early-morning buzz of the electric razor. As soon as
she hears it, she perks up and sharply eyes every move
of the Sovereign Pontiff.

In the tiny private chapel there is a stir: the Pope has
opened his bedroom door. A *cameriere secreto*, attired in
black and violet, bows his head in greeting. Two nuns
are kneeling at their beads. Lighted tapers flicker beneath the picture of the Holy Virgin. The Pope assumes
the alb, the stole, the chasuble; he steps up to the altar,
makes a sweeping sign of the cross, and in a low voice
begins the prayers of the Mass. Countless priests in thousands of churches, at this same hour and with these same
gestures, are murmuring these very prayers.

When Mass and the acts of grace have been concluded, the Pope goes to the dining room where he has
his solitary meals: protocol no longer admitting that anyone, no matter who, shall partake at the pontifical table.
His first meal of the day is a frugal one, according to the

custom of the Mediterranean lands. However, in the Vatican's huge bakery where the work goes on all through the night, the Sister in charge, an hour since, has painstakingly selected for him the small loaf that has turned out lightest, with the most golden-brown and crackly crust. The Pope eats his breakfast at the same hour of the day as the curates and vicars in every parish the world over. And, like them, he is mulling over the long day's work that lies ahead.

After glancing quickly through some half-dozen newspapers—Italian, French, American, English, German, Spanish—he rises, repeats the *Deo gratias*, and leaves his apartment. The Swiss Guards in the vast outer hall bend the knee and a footman in scarlet livery opens the door of the lift. The Pope descends to the second floor, makes his way into the private library, and picks up the telephone that connects him by direct wire with the office of the Pro-Secretary of State. From that moment the plain, humble, and retired existence of the private apartment is broken off. The sovereign who reigns over four hundred and fifty million subjects begins his working day.

III

Over Earth and Over Heaven . . .

THE POPE, ON THIS PAR-
ticular morning, will not remain long at his desk. Ahead
of him lies the ceremonial of a canonization at St. Peter's.
If he were still at leisure to cross over to the window, he
would behold the huge square in front of the basilica

seething with humanity. Detachments of pontifical gendarmes and guards palatine already are at their posts at the foot of the cathedral square. A group of breathless seminarians are trying to force their way through and one can sense that the basilica is jammed with a buzzing throng.

The Master of Ceremonies, opening the door part way, now quietly signals to the Pope. Rising meekly, he proceeds with his customary rapid stride along the broad corridors of the Vatican, answering with a benediction the salute of the Swiss Guards. In the halls adjoining the Sistine Chapel a small crowd of dignitaries awaits him. Only the murmur of the prelates breaks the silence as the Pope is vested with the robes of state. Heavy and gold-embroidered, the fabrics of silk and moire and stiff brocade blot out the simple white cassock. The slender hands that lately crumbled the plain breakfast loaf are encased in white silk gloves, upon one of which sparkles a magnificent ring.

The papal procession has already formed in front of the Sistine Chapel. The *sedia* is in readiness. Standing upon a sort of long litter, it is a tall armchair adorned with gold and upholstered in velours, and it is borne by twelve *sediari*. The Sovereign Pontiff ascends the portable throne and the *sediari*, arrayed in scarlet tunics, hoist it upon their shoulders. The procession gets under way in silence. High on his throne, swaying upon the shoulders of the bearers, the Pope gazes at the Royal Stairway of Bernini as it spreads away beneath him. The tiara, composed of three diadems set one upon another, weighs heavy on his head. The procession enters the basilica by way of the inner atrium and the air is split by a sudden blast of silver trumpets. The crowd responds with ap-

plause and ecstatic shouts. Impassive and rigidly aloof
beneath his heavy panoply of silks and precious stones,
the Sovereign Pontiff is wafted along above the crowd as
it acclaims him in a splendor of lights and music and
supplications.

The Pope, in proceeding with a canonization, is exercising the full plenitude of his powers, which this morning extend infinitely beyond the world of mortal men.
In proclaiming as a saint the young daughter of Latium
who was murdered by a sex fiend, Pius XII is about to
exercise a right of sovereignty not alone over the Church
Militant, which is the realm of flesh and blood, but over
the Church Triumphant, which consists of spirits unseen.
This morning, in St. Peter's, he stands at the summit of
his powers. Henceforth the faithful shall have the right
to place the image of this little Italian peasant girl upon
altars, and burn candles and incense before her, and in-
voke her intercession with solemn rites. For the Pope is
proclaiming that he has plumbed the mystery of this
particular human life; and he solemnly announces that
the new saint has now taken her place among the ranks
of the Elect in Heaven.

But, while it is true that every Pope proclaims saints,
Pius XII has seen fit to assert his powers in a most striking
fashion, and one that is rare in the whole history of the
Papacy. For he has "laid down" a dogma, promulgating
urbi et orbi the definition of an article of faith; and from
this day forward no Catholic may reject that article without falling into heresy and instantly ceasing to be a
member of the Church. When, with high pomp, in the
midst of St. Peter's Square, the Pope in 1950 solemnly
defined the dogma of the Assumption, he was ruling over
the consciences of men. He was affirming in the name of

the Church that at the death of the Virgin Mary, her body—her body, and not alone her soul—became present in Heaven, in a manner mysterious but perfectly real, at the side of her Son Jesus Christ; and that that body never had undergone such dissolution as the bodies of other mortals undergo. Once this dogma had been proclaimed, nothing thenceforward could throw doubt upon the Church's professed doctrine on this subject: for the Sovereign Pontiff is infallible. There was no further choice in the matter, there was no appeal from it—nor would there ever be, until the end of time. The decision was binding upon the Church of mortal men, upon the Church Militant and the Church Triumphant.

For a few moments, then, this humble old man was ruling over Heaven and earth. Who is the Pope?

IV

Doctrine and Dogma

＊

THE POPE, ACCORDING TO
Catholic dogma, is God's representative upon earth. He
is Vicar of Jesus Christ, he is visible Head of the Church;
and in Christ's name he can, under certain solemn circumstances, extend jurisdiction over the living and the

dead, thus establishing articles of faith for the Christian community both present and to come.

Here, in outline, is the constitution of the Church regarded as a mystical body which is composed of the departed, the living, and those yet to be born.

God is the creator of all things. His Son, Jesus Christ, was made flesh and became a man in order to accomplish the redemption of the human race through his own suffering and death. Christ is founder of the Church and forever remains its Head Invisible. He surrounds himself with Apostles. These are the forerunners of bishops; and the "prince" of the Apostles is Peter. Christ's word has designated Peter as Head of the disciples of the Church: "Thou art Peter [*Tu es Petrus*] and upon this rock I will build my Church. . . . Feed my sheep." Thus Peter becomes the first Pope. Transferring his residence to Rome, Peter makes it the capital city of the new universal empire, which is the empire of souls. He becomes Bishop of Rome. And ever since his martyrdom (which took place on the site of the present Basilica of St. Peter) the Bishops of Rome, following after him in a succession which has been unbroken for nearly two thousand years, have claimed it as their right to direct the Church.

The primacy of the Bishop of Rome has not gone uncontested. In the course of centuries there have been Churches which, refusing to recognize this primacy, have broken away from Rome: the Orthodox of the Eastern Church, gravitating about Byzantium and afterward about Moscow; and the Anglicans, the Calvinists, the Lutherans, the Zwinglian Protestants, and others. And today, behind the Iron Curtain, the Communist governments are attempting to stir up strife and schism among Catholics in their countries.

In spite of such defections, which from times past have drained away hundreds of millions of men, the Church of Rome has pursued the troubled course of its earthly existence; nor has it weakened the firm structure of its hierarchical organization. On the contrary—it has reinforced it unceasingly. Peter is perpetually at Rome. He is forever Prince of the Apostles; and his imperial sway over bishops, priests, and the faithful to whom he extends his jurisdiction is more undisputed than ever.

Century after century the Church has formulated the papal attributes in terms ever more precise. Under the two hundred and sixty-three pontificates that have made up the succession, the Popes have formed and dissolved alliances with the secular arm, and they have carried on struggles against emperors and a host of other temporal sovereigns. Eighty years have gone by since one of their number, Pope Pius IX, signalized the Church's defeat in the secular realm; for he lost Rome when it became the capital of modern Italy. But it was this same Pope who laid down the dogma proclaiming the supreme spiritual power of the Sovereign Pontiff: Infallibility. Thenceforth it became impossible to be a Catholic without believing that in certain very special circumstances, and under certain most definite conditions, the Pope can not err when he proclaims articles of faith.

Thus the Pope's power is above all a doctrinal power. He safeguards and defines the Church's teaching. And that is basic, for the strength of the Church is to be found in the intangibility of its doctrine. Inviolable it must be. No error, no transgression or act of rebellion is more grave than a revolt against the power of the Church's teaching—there is no more deadly sin than the sin of heresy. Communism, which so often endeavors to

present itself under the semblance of a religion, has its
own counterpart to this, for it dreads ideological "deviations" above all else.

Let it be perfectly clear, however, that the Pope never
invents or adds anything to the doctrine of the Church.
That doctrine has found expression once and for all,
first, through Revelation (which is to say, in Holy Scrip-
ture: the Old and New Testaments, the Epistles, the
Acts of the Apostles, and the Apocalypse), and thereafter through Tradition, by which is meant the aggregate
of the sayings and writings that form a running com-
mentary upon Revelation; the Church Fathers being its
main authors. When the Pope functions, then, as infallible
teacher, he does no more than single out, define, and
interpret a truth contained within the sum of truth
revealed. It is in this sense that the Pope is spoken of as
"defining" a particular truth *ex cathedra.*

In ages past, before the Pope had formulated this
definition, the Church used to meet in Ecumenical Councils; and there its doctrine was formulated and defended
by the assembled Fathers. But Councils of the Church
have become more and more infrequent—and meanwhile
the Popes have increasingly reserved to themselves the
sole right of proclaiming dogmas. They do so, however,
only after prolonged periods of advance study by theologians, and following consultation with the Church as a
whole. Thus, in respect of the doctrine of the Assumption proclaimed in 1950, several years had gone by since
Pius XII called upon a large number of specialists in
matters Marian to bring the formulation of the doctrine
to a head. Furthermore, the Pope had not been the prime
mover in this matter, which was initiated by a number of
theologians. Before proclaiming the doctrine, the Pope

had also sent out a lengthy questionnaire to all bishops, superiors of orders, and theologians of highest repute. This species of referendum showed that a great majority were in favor of the "definition." Thus, it was only after taking many precautions in regard to what might be called the public opinion of the Church that the Pope issued his definite pronouncement.

This particular dogma has brought forth numerous commentaries and has stirred up no little surprise, even shock in some quarters. It is nevertheless a fact that since the early centuries of the Church a special cult has centered about the Assumption of the Virgin. Numerous sanctuaries have been dedicated to it, Eastern as well as Western, and the iconography devoted to this article of faith is incalculable. Even so, the Popes waited nearly fifteen centuries before making a definitive pronouncement.

Popes are chary of exercising their privilege of infallibility. Four pontificates prior to that of Pius XII had gone by without the proclamation of new dogmas. Pius IX, on the other hand, promulgated two: the Immaculate Conception (1854) and Papal Infallibility (1870), and he also was the Pope who called the last Ecumenical Council to date, the Council of the Vatican. (That one was interrupted by political developments and was never reconvened.) Actually, the "articles of faith" that must be believed under pain of heresy are few in number. Yet those are the dogmas that form the base upon which the complex structure of Church doctrine stands.

V

Popes Have the Right To Be Wrong

THE GREATEST PLEASURE
one can give the Pope is to present him with a new dictionary. Pius XII is an avid collector of lexicons. Latest editions of the vocabularies of all the languages he speaks hold the place of honor on his library shelves. He is inces-

31

santly consulting and comparing these word lists and it
amuses him to detect flaws in the philological knowledge
of ambassadors or bishops whose native tongues he knows.
He takes the keenest pleasure, for example, in the battle
over vowel stress that has long divided the Portuguese
and Brazilians.

However, the Pope does not rest content with mastering
the grammatical niceties of the languages he keeps up
with. He is a student of their styles as well, and is familiar
with their literary classics. One of his advisers in French
usage is his long-time friend Monsignor Grente, a Member of the Academy, whom he has made a cardinal.

Bent low over the pages of his manuscript, Pius XII is
hard at work. He is preparing the discourse he will deliver
in a fortnight to the International Congress of Micro-
biologists and his desk is heaped with scientific works.
Faithful to his practice, he is getting down to the heart
of the subject; for he is anxious that when the audience
is over, the scientists who have gathered from every
quarter of the globe shall agree as to the precision of his
knowledge in their domain. The Pope does occasionally
call in advisers for the preparation of such an address,
but the main outline is his, he revises the draft himself,
and the Vatican Library often is obliged to send out
world-wide appeals in order to satisfy the bibliographical
demands of its most constant reader.

Pius XII likes to write only with the little nibs that
schoolboys once used, the steel ones, hard to come by
nowadays, that were made before the First World War.
Wherefore he is extremely fussy about taking care of his

pen, and at the end of the task he never neglects to wipe the point painstakingly with a bit of cloth. He writes his corrections in a small, tidy hand and types out the fair copy himself.

He has an extraordinary, photographic memory. All he has to do is read attentively twice through a script in order to learn it by heart; and then, when he delivers his discourse, every least peculiarity of the typing, every phrase written into the margin, every printed-in interpolation of the steel pen stands out like a guide mark along the way.

"When I am addressing a great crowd," Pius XII confided one day to a close friend, "nothing is able to distract me—the noise, the movement, nothing. I can see every page of my address. I have it photographed inside me and all I do is read." Since his last illness, however, he usually takes along the manuscript of his discourse and reads it.

The present Pope regards it as his main duty to receive everyone who requests an audience and to expound the views of the Head of the Church upon every subject, even the most worldly. And now that his advisers have decided upon the regular publication, in volumes, of his countless pronouncements, he never fails to sound out his listeners about technical errors which may have crept into his remarks, so as to be able to furnish the printers with a definitive text.

He makes a great many speeches. Not a day goes by without his delivering one or more discourses in several of the seven languages of which he has fluent command.

Whether he is addressing himself to dentists or midwives, to astronomers or bicycle racers, he is not satisfied merely to utter some generalized good advice but gives a precise description of his auditors' trade or profession and summarizes the advantages that proceed from it. He delivers himself in this way upon a wide variety of subjects: the benefits and dangers of sport; the care of the new-born; birth control; aspects of married life; the latest theories of light or techniques of dentistry; insurance, existentialism, the press, television, travel, histopathology, gastro-enterology, civil aviation. . . .

Not all Popes, by any means, have been thus ready to discuss the problems of the day, let alone the current ideologies and fads. But Pontiffs consistently have spoken out upon the great questions of their time. While refraining from intervention in the purely temporal sphere, they at all times claim the right to advise Catholics in every area where doctrine or morals are called in question—which is tantamount to saying, in every department of life.

The most impressive way in which a Pope can take a public stand (barring, of course, the infallible definition of dogma, which is extremely rare) is by means of an Encyclical. This is a letter written to all the faithful. Encyclicals are written in Latin, except in special cases when Popes may see fit to write directly in the speech of the land addressed. That was done, for instance, when Pius XI, writing an encyclical letter in condemnation of nazism, used German. Sovereign Pontiffs may write still other letters, more limited in scope, which are called "Bulls." When they utter allocutions *urbi et orbi* they are addressing themselves to the world at large. And lately, it has become traditional for them to receive countless pilgrims in audience.

From time to time, many Catholics are astounded or even shocked by some stand that is taken by the Head of the Church. These public declarations are not, as already noted, infallible. A Catholic who finds himself in disagreement with some opinion contained in a Papal allocution does not on that account fall into heresy. A tribunal of the Church has even been known to pronounce the Sovereign Pontiff in error.*

It is permissible for a Catholic to regard as open to question the specific political, economic, scientific, or esthetic pronouncements of the Supreme Pontiff and, more conclusively, of bishops. Apart from dogmas proclaimed *ex cathedra*, in short, a Pope's words and deeds fall within the sphere of everyday life and are to be gauged and assessed only in relation to their historical context. They are not binding upon the Catholic conscience. In the domain of relative values, then, even Popes have the right to be wrong. And yet . . .

---

* Mgr. A. Jullien, senior member of the Rota, relates that in its decision dated March 15, 1909, that tribunal found a verbal decision of Pius X to be not binding as against a vested interest which his interlocutor had failed to mention.

VI

Disciplinary Powers

WHEN ONE HAS SAID,
"They are not binding upon the Catholic conscience,"
the statement calls at once for qualification. In brief, one
must distinguish between the acceptance of dogmas that
are expressed under the seal of infallibility and the

Catholic attitude toward opinions expressed by Popes in
the other manifestations of their authority. Dogmas are
the essential elements of Church doctrine. Catholic morality stems from them. It is simply the logical consequence which truth imposes upon the actions of men by
whom those dogmas are recognized. For Catholics, however, the Pope has attributes other than that of infallible
guardian of the true doctrine.

He is also *Head* of the Church, and as such he holds
disciplinary powers. As Vicar of Christ he is endued with
a power which is absolute and immediate. Every hierarchy upon the plane of things visible springs originally
from him, and he can at all times take the place of any
Church dignitary whatsoever and govern with full power
in his place and stead. Because he is first of the Apostles,
it is permitted him to legislate as of sovereign right.

Laymen and ecclesiastics, in their varying degrees, are
bound to recognize the Pope in his quality as Head. Those
who refuse him this obedience are schismatics. In the
eyes of the Church, theirs is a deviation far less heinous
than that of the heretics. For the latter deny the very
foundation of the Church: the unassailability of its doctrine. Thus it is that the Protestants, who have attacked
the basis of the Catholic creed, are heretics, whereas the
Greek and Russian Orthodox are—or were, at any rate,
at the moment of their separation—schismatics; for, while
refusing obedience to the Sovereign Pontiff, they nonetheless continued to regard the dogmas as articles of faith
and to observe the usage of the Sacraments.

Let us take the case of an individual. If a priest of the
Latin rite rebels against a Papal edict or breaks the law
of celibacy or persists, despite a formal interdiction from

Rome, in some political or social dispute, he becomes a schismatic. No matter how much notoriety or scandal his case may arouse, in the eyes of the Church it will always be a far less serious offense than that of the most obscure professor in some out-of-the-way seminary who assails Church doctrine itself.

Now, so far as laymen are concerned, the Pope's disciplinary power bears essentially upon the interpretation of doctrine. Interpretations of that sort are to be found in every word the Pope utters; and, depending upon their temperament, some Sovereign Pontiffs, as is true of Pius XII, express themselves freely upon every problem that confronts mankind. Others, like Pius X, rarely go outside the realm of things spiritual. The importance of the views expressed by Popes is in direct proportion to the universality of the discourse in which those opinions are uttered. One need hardly say that an address to a troop of Belgian Boy Scouts carries far less weight than an Encyclical. The latter serves to formulate a point of instruction in terms far too weighty to be simply rejected out of hand by any Catholic, whether clerical or lay, without risk of becoming a schismatic.

On the other hand, it does not follow that that instruction shall be binding upon conscience: that the Catholic is under obligation to regard it as an article essential to his faith. He may accede to it only by virtue of the bond of discipline uniting him to the Head of the Church. Encyclicals are almost always prompted by the problems of the day, and they become outdated as those problems do likewise. Leo XIII, in 1893, was a pioneer of social reform. His Encyclical of that year was a sensation, causing horror in the ranks of the genteel. The world, however, moved; and other Encyclicals, to meet changing situations, have enlarged upon and clarified the Church's present-day thinking about those same problems.

In thus staking out the main guideposts of Catholic thought, the Pope is not alone. He has at hand to assist him a body which is specifically entrusted with the safeguarding of the Church's doctrine. This is that bureau of Church government which goes by the name of Congregation of the Holy Office; and it publishes solemn decrees which clarify the Church's teaching or condemn some particular theory. The layman, by virtue of the bond of discipline, is in duty bound to pay heed to these decrees, but he may submit them to the judgment of his conscience and is permitted to criticize their premises as debatable. In matters of doctrinal interpretation the final word belongs, however, to the Church hierarchy and the Pope.

Part Two

HIERARCHY AND BISHOPS

VII

The Hierarchy and Freedom

CLERICS ARE LINKED TO
the Pope with much tighter bonds than laymen. They are
like soldiers, in that they never question discipline. The
chain of command of this army, which is composed entirely of volunteers, is simple in the extreme. The hier-

archy is organized upon three levels—priests, bishops, and
the Pope. The faithful enrolled under them go to make
up, in the normal course, the membership of the basic
administrative unit, which is the parish. This in turn is
one component in the organization of the diocese. And the
diocese ties directly in with Rome.

In this way the Church has its members in charge from
birth to death. The parish priest baptizes the parishioner,
instructs him, administers the Sacraments to him, succors
him in the hour of death, and consecrates his grave. And
beyond the grave that man is still a member of the
Church, though now no longer of the Church Militant,
as when here upon earth, but of the Church Suffering
(Purgatory) and then of the Church Triumphant, in
Heaven. Of this mystical body, composed of the living
and the dead, the Head is the founder of the Church,
Jesus Christ.

The Church Militant, which is a visible association, is
controlled by Christ's representative upon earth, the
Pope. The guiding lines all lead to Rome. The parish
priest is answerable to his bishop and the bishop to the
Pope. Monks and nuns of all the religious orders are
linked to Rome in a manner which is different but none
the less real. Certain of the orders are outside the bishop's
jurisdiction—and their superiors are responsible directly
to the Pope. And lastly, in the mission field or in lands
where religious persecution is rife, it is not possible for
Catholics to be organized according to the usual ascend-
ing scheme. Their dependence, instead, is upon the Congregation of the Propagation of the Faith (the Secretariat
of Missions) or the Congregation for the Eastern Church,
the latter of which has under its jurisdiction the greater
part of those Catholics who are behind the Iron Curtain.

When one takes into account, moreover, the fact that Rome's latest regulations require every Western diocese to duplicate, in its internal organization, the main aspects of the Roman Curia, one is bound to remark not only the essential unity of the Church as a whole, but also the striving toward centralization that has gone on during recent pontificates.

I have now given a bare outline of the hierarchical system, thanks to which the Church assures its administrative unity and the discipline that unites the whole body of the faithful to parish priests, the bishops, and the Pope. But, howsoever firm may be the ties that bind every individual member to the visible society which is the Church Catholic, that body also claims to be a community of far greater breadth and depth in the realm of the purely spiritual. It is that community which is implicit in the expression, the "Soul of the Church."* To this higher communion one gains access through personal acceptance alone, by an exercise of free will. Or, to put it another way, the hierarchical structure of the Church in no wise limits the personal freedom of its members; quite the contrary. The essential principle of the Church's whole morality is, that a person must act always according to his conscience and in perfect freedom. It follows that the Catholic discipline is of no avail unless it is freely subscribed to. The essential freedom of man, not only in his relationship to all other men but in relation to God himself, is a dogma of Catholicism. It is one of the dogmas that divide it, for instance, from Lutheran Protestantism, since, according to the latter, Divine Grace is omnipotent.

However, in everyday life, priests, and more especially

---

* See the final chapter.

those who are educators, do not always escape the temptation to exercise spiritual pressure. In the extremely delicate intercourse that takes place between a trusting soul and a spiritual director or judge, there is need of great adroitness, and even more of strong inner discipline, if there is to be guidance without warping or bruising.

On the other hand, if a Catholic, going beyond all injunctions, refers his case to the Pope as supreme judge, he will always find in the Sovereign Pontiff the defender of the human spirit's essential freedom. This freedom it is that shall prevail over every injunction, even though imposed by the highest authorities of the Church. The rule of conscience is the highest law, according to Catholic theology.

Take marriage, for example. The Church maintains the indissolubility of that bond in the strongest possible terms. But if one party to the contract can prove before the tribunal of the Rota that he was not entirely free at the moment he received that Sacrament—that he was deprived of full freedom of choice by some coercion exercised upon him—Rome will not hesitate to declare the marriage null and void.

Or, again, take the priesthood. If a regularly ordained priest can prove to the Pope that pressure was brought to bear upon him, coercing him into taking Holy Orders without vocation, he can thereupon secure release from his vows. He will not stop being a priest, for he has received a Sacrament which nothing can set aside; but he may follow the pursuits of a layman and he may marry without thereby cutting himself off from the Church.

VIII

Ministry of the Interior

I WAS CLINGING TO THE platform of one of those overloaded buses that plow breakneck back and forth along the congested streets of the Trastevere. Perched beside me on the same step, swaying to and fro at every twist of the zigzag alleys

47

teeming with children and dogs and pushcarts, clung an
elderly clergyman. Then the conductor demanded our
fares and our toehold became even more precarious. The
old priest, whom I took for a country curate, worried off
his threadbare glove. On his finger there gleamed a
splendid amethyst. He was a bishop, hurrying to attend a
Papal audience.

He was not the only bishop of the bus routes; and I
had lately observed a pair of others, having a meal at
Alfredo the Pasta King's. At the Ciampino airdrome, too,
they are often to be seen, dressed in plain clerical garb,
their episcopal rings agleam in the sunshine of the Roman
Campagna.

Rome swarms with bishops. But in the Eternal City
they lose the majesty of bearing that distinguishes them
in their cathedral towns. The blasé Romans jostle them
in the streets. In keeping with their circumstances, which
often are quite pinched, they put up at a hospitable religious house or some monastery in the suburbs, or at a
seminary. Those coming from more prosperous lands take
a room at the Hotel Minerva, traditionally reserved for
ecclesiastics only. Cardinal Spellman, Archbishop of New
York, is faithful to the Grand Hotel and holds press
conferences there.

But no matter how lowly or even how poverty-stricken
bishops may sometimes appear, they are "brothers of the
Pope"; direct descendants, all, of the Apostles who were
the founding fathers of the Church. The Pope, enthroned
at the Eternal City and successor to St. Peter, retains the
full plenitude of power. In many respects, though, the
bishops are his peers. Each is possessed of sovereign
powers in his own diocese. "Aside from the plenary and

supreme jurisdiction exercised by the Sovereign Pontiff over the Church Universal, the individual Church, through and in its bishop, is possessed of the whole mystery of Christ in fullest life, together with every good and divine gift that the Church Universal possesses." (Monsignor Guerry.)

It has taken nearly two millenia for the Church to establish its system of government. Even so, the ticklish problem of *de facto* relations between Pope and bishop still is not resolved. No shadow of doubt exists, to be sure, when it comes to a question of infallible definitions: only the Pope has that power. But, wherever the powers of Church government are concerned, the two authorities proceed with circumspection side by side and, in some sectors, with mutual interference.

Small wonder that the Communist governments are so hostile to Catholic bishops. They well know that the Church's sole possibility of survival rests in the bishops' hands. The mainstay of Catholicism is the Apostolic Succession. Monsignor Dupont, a French bishop, and Monsignor Wu Pak Chu, a Chinese, are the direct successors of the Apostles and their disciples. And this succession, the Church holds, has come down unbroken. The Jewish fishermen who were Jesus' disciples appointed their successors by the ritual laying-on of hands. Generation after generation, this gesture of consecration has been passed along. And the bishop, for his part, is charged with the ordaining of priests. There can be no priests without bishops. Without bishops, there can be no Church. And that is why, behind the Iron Curtain, every effort is being made to find bishops who would be agreeable to turning their backs on Rome, but who would go on ordaining priests in a manner recognized as valid by Rome and parishioner alike. Defections have been few—Rome does not pick diocesans with her eyes closed—and the Communists have almost everywhere failed to establish congregations of Catholic schismatics.

How then does the Pope, as commander-in-chief, make certain of liaison between his Vatican headquarters and the bishops; and how, upon occasion, does he exercise supervision?

He does so primarily with the help of the Consistorial Congregation, which serves the Church, to all practical purposes, as Ministry of the Interior. The Consistory, as it is called for convenience, is responsible for making periodical surveys of the management of every Western diocese. (The Eastern Catholic Church is supervised by the Congregation bearing that name.)

Rome goes about this in two ways. The bishops are in duty bound to render a highly detailed report to the Consistory, every five years, in reply to a questionnaire, the main heads of which will be presented in a moment.* And bishops are required, moreover, to report to Rome in person for what is called the visit *ad limina*. Only by special authorization can a bishop be dispensed from making this visit to the Pope and to his "Minister of the Interior." The rotation according to which every bishop's report must be made to Rome has been permanently fixed. First year: Italy, Corsica, Sardinia, Sicily, Malta. Second year: Spain, Portugal, France, Belgium, Holland, England, Scotland, Ireland. Third year: the rest of Europe. Fourth year: the Americas. Fifth year: Africa, Asia, Australia.

---

* We are indebted for this outline to Monsignor Martin's excellent book, *Les Congrégations Romaines.*

The questionnaire sent out to every bishop by the Consistory is in twelve parts and is written in Latin. Here is a summary of it:

I.—*General Information:* Name, age, place of origin, bishop's exact address, date of consecration; historical account of the diocese, its extent, climate, language, total population, proportion of Catholics to members of dissident sects, etcetera.

II.—*Temporal:* Under what system of civil tenure is the ecclesiastical property held and what is the source of the clergy's income; and does the bishop have an administrative council? Does he follow their advice; and who are the members? Are the provisions of canon law observed in regard to records of receipts and expenditures, civil procedures, etcetera? How are offerings administered; collections; Mass fees? Is there a detailed inventory of property, real and other, appertaining to every person of trust; and what measures are taken to avoid risk of loss or misappropriation in the event that a parish priest or other administrative officer absconds?

III.—*Faith and Worship:* Errors and superstitions common to the diocese; and do they affect the clergy? What degree of freedom of worship is allowed by civil law and by hostile elements of the population?

IV.—*The Bishop:* Income from the episcopal allotment, real property, State subvention, etcetera. Does it suffice? Has the diocese any debts; and what steps are being taken to clear them? Condition of the Episcopal Palace; and its personnel in detail? How does the bishop maintain his residence? How often does he preach, write pastoral letters, pontificate, confirm? How many priests has he ordained during the past five years? How closely does he follow the prescribed procedures relative to episcopal

administration? (The questionnaire goes into the point
in great detail.) What are his relations with the civil
authorities?

V.—*The Diocesan Staff:* Real property and financial resources of the various departments; full list of functionaries. Personal estimates of the vicars general and of
their work.

VI.—*The Seminary:* Intellectual and moral condition?
Is care exercised to train the students in professional
conduct and good manners?

VII.—*The General Clergy:* Have they enough to live
on? How is provision made for the aged and infirm?
Does the diocese own a house of retreat for its clergy;
for its priests under penance? What is the behavior of
the clergy (give details)? To how many priests has the
bishop granted permission to engage in banking, co-
operatives, labor organizations, other social agencies? Attitude of the clergy toward the bishop; toward the Holy
See. Do any priests write for newspapers? Is their activity
in that field beneficial? Has the bishop been compelled to
assign canonical penalties and with what result?

VIII.—*The Chapter:* Number of canons and dignitaries,
etcetera. . . .

IX.—*The Religious:* Is the bishop careful to visit houses
of religion every five years? Are there monks or nuns not
living the life conventual? What is their reputation?

X.—*Congregations:* State of morals generally. Of family
life. Is the religious spirit superficial or devout? Are children baptized immediately? Are communions made frequently? Percentage of civil marriages, free unions, civil
interments. Are these last the result of too high diocesan
assessments? What training do children receive, home as
well as school? Number and usefulness of associations
and confraternities. State the situation in regard to secret

or anticlerical societies. Are Catholics attentive to their
duties as Catholics in their participation in political affairs . . . ?

And thus the Pope is able, at any moment and in the
most minute detail, to know what is going on in every
Catholic diocese, without exception, throughout the
world.

The information reaching the Holy See from all parts
of the Catholic domain is often spot-checked by visitors
who arrive from Rome. In countries where the Sovereign
Pontiff maintains official representatives, reports also are
checked by the nuncios. These emissaries, who serve as
ambassadors, have a triple function: to represent the
Pope *vis-à-vis* the national government and the local hierarchy, and to keep the Holy See informed about the
status of the Catholic Church in the lands to which they
are accredited. And lastly, the Vatican is a place of call
on the itineraries of a great many travelers, dozens of
whom are received in personal audience by the Holy
Father every day. Visits of this sort are worked up in
advance; and from such conversations, in the course of
which the Pope asks many questions but contributes few
remarks, he receives essential supplementary information.
It is on this basis that he proceeds to sound out public
opinion. Nor does the Pope see only ecclesiastics in these
interviews. He also receives many laymen, organizers of
Catholic Action groups, deputations, non-Catholic political leaders, and sometimes his opponents.

Finally, there is at Rome a sort of secondary Ministry
of the Interior, the Congregation of the Religious, assigned to supervision of those living the "regular" life:

the monks and nuns who form so large a part of the Church's ranks. Just as the Consistory attempts to curb the independence of the bishops, so the Congregation of the Religious endeavors to bridge over the intervals resulting from the too great autonomy of the various orders. Through this agency, highly detailed reports come into Rome concerning the life of the conventual establishments. The process is not an easy one, for the Benedictines, Dominicans, Franciscans, Jesuits, Carmelites, Oratorians, and a host of other religious orders all have highly prized secular traditions which they strive patriotically, as it were, to maintain in an effort to avoid uniformity. In addition to its own rule of life, each of the great orders has its peculiar forms of worship, its *mystique,* and its own philosophy. Regarded as privileges most jealously to be preserved are the nomination or election of superiors and their autonomy within the orders themselves.

The internal organization of the orders is highly diverse. The Benedictines are broken up into numerous abbeys, each independent of the rest but joined in a federation, and all living under the Rule laid down by St. Benedict. The Dominicans are under the jurisdiction of a Master General residing at Rome, and are grouped into various provinces. Among the Jesuits, centralization is carried even further. They likewise have a general who is resident at Rome, and his authority over every member of the order is comparable to that of an absolute monarch. But, whether the orders constitute federations of "autonomous" communities or whether they form a single army under command of a general vested with fullest authority, they all wish to follow their own rules of life and they strive to preserve their independence from the centralized administration of the Church. It is against this tendency that the Congregation of the Religious bends its efforts. And through this agency it is that the Popes, pursuing their policy of centralization, seek to extend Rome's control into the very heart of the closest conventual order.

The Congregation of the Religious sends questionnaires to the superior of every order, just as the Consistory does to every bishop. In addition, the Congregation specifically requests the superiors and other dignitaries of the orders to supply it, by means of "confidential" letters, with all sorts of supplementary information. Every five years, exactly as under the Consistory, superiors are required to submit a highly detailed report on the order and its members; on the financial condition of the convents; on the existing state of relations between the houses of religion and the bishop, the confessors, the almoners. In the questionnaire addressed to the sisterhoods occur queries such as these:

"In the event of a sister leaving the order, has the full sum of the dowry been returned, regardless of its character, and likewise the trousseau, supposing the sister to have brought one? If there was no dowry and the person in question had no personal resources, did the house provide her, of its charity, with the means of returning safely to her home and there decently residing for some while?"

Nor does the Congregation neglect to ask whether "the superior or the bursar have disposition of secret funds, the disposal of which does not figure on the books."

Part Three

WHEELS WITHIN WHEELS

His Holiness, Pope Pius XII

The Most Reverend Monsignor Domenico Tardini

IX

Within the Private Apartment

THIS FRAIL MAN, INFAL-
lible guardian of the Church's doctrine and absolute ruler
over 450 millions of the devout, has no heir apparent, no
Secretary of State, no confidant. Dwelling in a vast palace
and surrounded with courtly pomp, he leads the life of a
solitary ascetic.

Every evening, when his long day's work is accomplished, he withdraws to the private apartment.

The apartment is a modern one. It has been done over in the slightly Germanic taste favored by Pius XII. The walls throughout are stipple-finished and every room is painted a different color: the chapel in light green, the bedroom plain white. The suite is broken up into many small rooms: bedroom, dining room, study, bath, and a number of sitting rooms where are displayed the many presents that come to the Holy Father from all quarters of the Catholic world. Pius XII does have a radio but he never uses it except to listen to the music of his favorite composers, Chopin and Mendelssohn, or to news reports.

A small inner stairway leads to the floor beneath, where the Pope's two archivists do their secretarial work. Both are Jesuits and both German, Father Leiber and Father Hendrich. At the far end of the suite is the kitchen, equipped with a gas stove, and there is also a small dining room and a dormitory set apart for Mother Pasqualina and the three Bavarian nuns who attend to the housekeeping under her direction.

The Pope is by himself. He has just had his dinner: a scant serving of meat and a few vegetables, a glass of wine, a cup of herb tea. Now he is attentively reading the *Osservatore Romano*. The sheets of the spread-out newspaper are slashed all over with pencil marks—all six pages of the Holy See's unofficial Italian-language daily will soon be covered with them. Pius XII reads the *Osservatore* line by line, from the reports of pontifical audiences straight through the death notices.

Suddenly the Pope reaches for the telephone (a pretentious gadget, all white and gold, presented by an American firm to his predecessor) and puts in a call for Professor Lolli. This man, cheerfully ironic and portly, rates the title of Pontifical Editor and is responsible for all news items having to do with the Sovereign Pontiff. It now appears that in the text of the Pope's address to the bicycle racers, the omission of a comma has changed the meaning of a sentence. The Holy Father is greatly upset. Whenever the *Osservatore* prints a Papal pronouncement ("precisely as, to the best of our ability, we gathered it from the august lips of His Holiness," to quote the time-honored phrase), Pius XII demands to see proofs and corrects them himself.

Long years before he became Pope, close associates of Cardinal Pacelli knew and dreaded this respect for commas and reverence for correct form. As Papal Secretary of State, he often made them copy a letter or dispatch six or seven times over.

His reading of the newspaper is interrupted by Commendatore Stefanori, his valet. He has come to announce a caller whose name does not appear in the audience list. It is one of the extremely small number of persons who have the privilege of calling upon the Holy Father without his summons—Count Galeazzi, the engineer who is a great financial expert and half-brother to the Pope's physician. Count Galeazzi is director of public works in the

little State. He is also an informed and entertaining conversationalist. Pius XII and the Count (whose title was
conferred upon him by the Italian Government between
the two wars, after a discreet hint from the Holy See)
start conversing upon a wide variety of topics. After deal-
ing briefly with a few Vatican City problems, they pass
to the important events of the day and then plunge into
the news of Rome itself: ambassadors and the problems
of ministries, the doings of society, a cardinal's anxieties,
a bishop's hopes.

Now Mother Pasqualina comes softly into the room.
Giving the Pope one of those quick and searching glances
with which nurses scrutinize the tender objects of their
care, she breaks in upon the conversation:

"The Holy Father is tired," she murmurs smilingly to
the Count.

Mother Pasqualina is the only person alive who could
venture such a familiarity. Etiquette, for her, simply does
not exist. Thirty years have passed since this Bavarian nun
entered the Pope's service, back in the far-off days when
Monsignor Pacelli was Nuncio to Germany. She has
watched over him ever since, following him first to the
Secretariat of State and then to the pontifical apartments.
She is a pious, sturdy woman, with a good head and
strong common sense. She is perfectly selfless; and she
understands the Pope better than anyone else, and is
able to gauge precisely how much work or fasting he can
endure. Mother Pasqualina anticipates his every need;
and, if occasion requires, she is always there at hand
with her blend of devotion and German *gemütlichkeit*.
She it is who lends to this enormous marble labyrinth a
touch of familiar warmth. It would otherwise be uninhab-
itable.

The visitors who enter the tiny domain under Mother Pasqualina's pious charge are few and far between. There is Prince Carlo Pacelli, one of the Holy Father's nephews, who is administrator of Vatican City; and there are the two Jesuit Fathers, Leiber and Hendrich, who are the Pope's routine assistants and collaborate with him in the working-up of many of his discourses. The part these two Fathers play in the Pope's intimate circle has often been greatly exaggerated. They are not always involved in top-secret matters but they do serve their order as an important link between the Jesuits and the Supreme Head of the Church. They also furnish Pius XII with a great deal of information regarding political and religious affairs in their native Germany. Once in a while, too, Signor Gedda, who is president of Catholic Action in Italy, enters the door of the private apartment. When Cardinal Spellman comes to Rome, he customarily avails himself of an evening call. Lastly, the Pope's confessor, the Reverend Father Bea, S.J., calls regularly at the apartment; and then for a few moments the Head of the Church becomes a humble penitent, no different from the lowliest of the low as he kneels before the priest who stands as judge in God's name.

Sober and frugal though it always is, Pius XII's private life is reduced to the extremest of simplicity during his long sojourns at his villa, Castelgandolfo, a few miles from Rome. Back in the time of Pius XI the whole Court used to move out to the summer palace, but nowadays only a corporal's guard of the Swiss go along when the Pope takes up residence there. The *cameriere secreto* who is prelate in attendance upon the Pope during audiences comes out from Rome and returns in the afternoon. There then remain in the huge domicile (apart from Mother Pasqualina, of course, and her three sisters) a handyman, serving as chauffeur and butler, and a young Vatican civil employee who does duty as valet de chambre. But both men go off duty at nightfall.

Supposing you were to slip through the thin cordon of Swiss Guards and make your way to the Pope's private quarters and press the doorbell, it would eventually be answered by the Sovereign Pontiff himself.

Such, then, is the tiny world wherein the Pope spends the few hours he allots to his private life. Farther off, outside the impenetrable circle, live and work the Pope's two chief collaborators, the heads of the State Secretariat. Remoter still are the Curia, the Court, and the Pacelli family.

X

Monsignor Inside and Monsignor Outside

ON THE FEAST OF THE
Epiphany, 1955, Giovanni Battista Montini, Archbishop
of Milan, made his solemn entry into his see city. At the
boundary of his archdiocese, the most important in all
Italy, he was met the night before by a delegation of

civil and ecclesiastical officials. The new archbishop thereupon stepped from his car and, walking forward a short way into the night, fell upon his knees in the snow and fervently kissed the land over which he was coming to preside.

This gesture symbolic of humility was followed next day by the ceremonial pomp of his installation at the Duomo of Milan and his ascent to the throne of St. Ambrose. And so, right in the public eye, came abruptly to an end the Roman career of Monsignor Montini, plain priest, who for years, in the shadow of the Pope, had served as Pro-Secretary of State for Internal Affairs and Pius XII's closest assistant.

At fifty-nine he looks not a day over forty. He is tall, balding, rather slight, with swarthy complexion and a burning glance, his brow creased by two deep vertical lines which lend a touch of severity to a countenance otherwise open and readily smiling. His priestly vocation came late. During the years of turmoil that followed World War I, G. B. Montini was active in Catholic organization work among Italian students. Those groups, known as the FUCI, have furnished most of the leaders for Catholic Action in Italy, and for the Christian-Democratic Party of today. While reading for his bar examinations at Rome, young Montini became deeply absorbed in the social problems of the epoch. But then, just as a challenging political future seemed to be opening before him—it was at the time when fascism was on the rise and its struggle with the other parties was growing bitter—he renounced the world and entered the Ecclesiastical Academy, the vocational school for the Vatican diplomatic corps. He passed almost immediately into the State Secretariat, where he mounted steadily from rung to rung of the service ladder, remaining all the while within the department itself except for a brief assignment to Poland.

However, he neglected no opportunity to escape from the dreary corridors of the State Secretariat, with its stuffy offices and the circumscribed concerns of its slightly unrealistic world. Montini went out preaching retreats for young students and spreading the doctrine through the purlieus of Rome. Meanwhile fascism had taken over the country and relegated Catholic Action to the domain of the strictly spiritual. Former students still recall the ascetic face and glowing eyes of Montini the preacher and counselor, and his deep, vibrant voice. Perhaps it was his long term of service in the State Secretariat which cooled his ardor and masked his passions behind a screen of diplomatic reserve.

Of his own accord, Monsignor Montini adopted the practice, from which he has rarely deviated, of never uttering a personal opinion or committing himself on any public issue. What he chose to be was a shadow—the shadow of the Pope. In so doing, he followed the example set by the man who was his preceptor in the art of Church government, none other than Cardinal Pacelli himself, when Pius XI appointed him Secretary of State. For Cardinal Pacelli preferred not to emulate his illustrious predecessors, a Consalvi or a Gasparri. What the Pope really required, so it seemed to him, was not such men as they had been but someone who would wholly identify himself with the Sovereign Pontiff's policies and carry them out to the letter.

Pius XI's successor, in any event, would admit of nothing else. Pius XII is a reserved man, slow to make up his mind, brusquely obstinate, mild in manner but easily put

out; and what he demands of his associates is that they
keep him posted, not advised. He wishes to know what
people's reactions are, and what are the trends of Catholic
opinion. Contrary to tradition, the Pope did not name a
new Secretary of State when Cardinal Maglione died.
The daily, even hourly cooperation between Pius XII and
Monsignor Montini thus became complete.

And yet, during his serious illness at the close of 1954
and the beginning of 1955, it was at the moment when
the Pope's vitality was at its lowest—when his life was
despaired of, and, lonely and apparently dying, Pius XII
seemed more than ever to need the support of the few
associates in whom he placed full trust—that he decided
to part with Monsignor Montini. The Pope designated him
archbishop and sent him to Milan—a see which traditionally carries with it the right to a cardinal's hat.

In well-informed circles, nobody had the slightest
doubt but that this amounted to a heroic decision on the
enfeebled Pontiff's part. And a considerable segment of
Catholic opinion saw in it an expression *in extremis* of
the Pope's desire not only to pave the way into the
Sacred College for Monsignor Montini, but also to provide him with a short cut back into the exercise of those
pastoral functions from which, in the course of his long
years of service with the State Secretariat, he had been
isolated. Some even went so far as to speculate that the
ailing Pope considered it advisable that Monsignor Montini, already familiarized under his tutelage with the
wheels within wheels governing the Church Universal,
should be brought in touch, through spiritual direction of
a great industrial city like Milan, with the down-to-earth
problems of the moment. And thus, in the company of his

peers of the Sacred College, he would one day find himself the richer for two kinds of experience and ready to assume the highest of dignities.

At Monsignor Montini's side and charged with responsibility for the Church's foreign policy, there has labored for many years in the State Secretariat another man, Monsignor Domenico Tardini. The two Pro-Secretaries of State complemented each other; and between them they ably seconded the labors of the Pope, whose basic requirement is that his entourage shall include a small number of assistants whom he has known long and well. Since his colleague's departure, Monsignor Tardini has been solely responsible to the Pope, who continues in poor health, for full conduct of both departmental sections. As a working arrangement, however, a younger prelate, long trained by Monsignor Montini himself, has succeeded him as head of Internal Affairs. He is Monsignor Angelo dell'Acqua, and he bears the title of Substitute.

The jovial Monsignor Tardini is as much a man of the south as his erstwhile colleague Montini is northern, and the two are antithetical in every way. Diplomat to his fingertips though he is, Monsignor Tardini is not a man to mince words, nor does he observe the niceties of protocol except on those very rare occasions when he receives a rank outsider in his enormous office. Whereas Monsignor Montini, toiling on and on, prolonged interviews regardless of mealtimes, his successor quits precisely on the stroke of one-thirty. Uncertain health (he

has liver trouble) is in part responsible for this adherence
to strict routine.

Short, peppery, and pug-nosed, with thick iron-gray
hair and owlish eyeglasses, Monsignor Tardini is obviously finding the double load now reposed on him hard
to bear. Surrounded by the excessive ceremonial of the
Vatican, he gives the impression of recoiling instinctively,
as if with a sort of startled amusement, from contact with
anything pompous, and he takes refuge in the deepest
humility every time some fresh honor comes his way.
What is now in store for him is the purple, which he has
already once declined. But it is hard to see how he can
escape it at some Consistory in the near future.

Monsignor Tardini does not dwell in the Holy Father's
immediate neighborhood as Montini did. He has a comfortable suite, formerly occupied by a diplomat, in a
modern apartment house on the farther side of Vatican
City. And Monsignor Tardini's thoughts are engrossed
by a sacred responsibility in addition to the cares of his
lofty post. There is an orphanage which he has founded
out of his own small resources and the sums he tirelessly
solicits from all who come to his office or whom he meets
in the salons of the Roman aristocracy; and he goes to
visit his little orphans every day. Casting aside his grave
responsibilities, he is then like a child among the children,
and he becomes once more a priest of souls as he listens
to those who bring him their problems of conscience or
their griefs.

XI

Problems of State

WHY, THOUGH, DID THE
State Secretariat find itself thus deprived of its normal
chief, the Cardinal-Secretary of State?

Some sixteen years ago a Conclave was held to elect a new
Pope. One cardinal stood far above the rest in prestige

and world acclaim: Eugenio Pacelli. But the Italian cardinals, who formed the majority of the Sacred College,
were by no means all in favor of his election. Pacelli's
candidacy did have, however, the support of a zealous
contingent. Chief among these were Cardinals Canali,
Marchetti-Selvaggiani, Pizzardo, and Tedeschini. There
was also the longtime Nuncio to Paris, Maglione. Eugenio
Pacelli was elected; and it would appear that he felt
morally obligated to appoint as director of the Church's
foreign affairs an experienced diplomat—and one, moreover, who had contributed so much toward his elevation
to the throne of St. Peter. Cardinal Maglione was named
Secretary of State. (We shall have more to say, later on,
about some of the Pope's other backers.)

The new Sovereign Pontiff was himself a departmental
career man. His entire experience had been gained at the
State Secretariat and through several important nuncia-
tures (notably, to Munich in 1917 and Berlin in 1920),
and he was Cardinal-Secretary of State at the time the
Conclave made him Pope. Now, this election ran contrary
to a tradition of long standing; for it was a high-policy
rule that the chief of the Church's political bureau never
should become supreme head. Finding himself elevated
to power at that moment of historical crisis, however, on
the eve of World War II, the new Pope, by temperament
an authoritarian and centralizer, was neither able nor
willing to give up his direct control of the Holy See's top
policy-making agency. Except for Maglione's brief tenure
at the Vatican, Pius XII has been Secretary of State without
interruption ever since his predecessor upon the throne
of St. Peter appointed him to that post long ago.

Is it a good thing or is it disadvantageous that all the
innumerable threads linking Catholicism to its world

capital should be thus gathered into the hands of one man? Quite possibly it was necessary to impose upon the Church this unity of direction, somewhat tortuous though it had upon occasion shown itself to be, at a period when conflicting forces of such magnitude were loose in the world and rushing headlong into an apocalyptic struggle. Indeed, it was because the world situation, and more especially the impending outbreak of war, overtopped all other anxieties, that the Sacred College had so quickly reached agreement upon the election of a man widely experienced in the conduct of foreign policy.

Be that as it may, the lack of a Cardinal-Secretary of State has met in Rome with criticism which continues to this day, more than a decade later. The inhuman burden of the work itself delayed its execution and held up the making of vital decisions. Certain problems of intrinsic importance were obviously being sidetracked in favor of other and more pressing ones, simply for want of time and physical strength. Little by little, the bureaus of the State Secretariat have seen their work enlarged out of all proportion; and this the Curia does not like. Since the elevation of Pius XII the State Secretariat has increasingly gained the right to supervise the work of the Congregations (which themselves are Ministries of State) and to intervene almost as a matter of course between them and the ranks of the devout, and between them and the Pope. Even before he was taken ill, Pius XII had systematically cut down contacts between himself and his heads of department, without granting any proportionate increase of independence of action on their part. The little book of "Audiences of Tabella," which is put out annually in great style by the *Maître de Chambre* to His Holiness, has shrunk to half the size it used to be, a few years back.

Audiences of Tabella, a routine fixture of the Pope's schedule, are interviews reserved to the heads and chief functionaries of the Congregations, presidents of ecclesiastical tribunals, and the like. Of late years, though, and long before his health was impaired, the Pope would often send word to prelates who were due to call upon him, asking them, since he had no questions to raise, to address themselves instead to the State Secretariat. Heads of missions accredited to the Holy See had numerous difficulties, too, on account of the absence of a Secretary of State. The high officials upon whom they paid their calls were not, so they found, empowered to make decisions but had to limit themselves to taking all requests under advisement, pending reference to higher quarters still.

Monsignor Tardini has for many years been head of the first section of the State Secretariat. Called the bureau for External Affairs, it is the most important section by virtue both of seniority and the scope of the problems with which it deals; and it is manned by a small staff, a mere fifteen prelates, all Italians and all of them highly experienced. Here is where contact is maintained with the nuncios, and to this section come all strictly political matters presented by chiefs of missions to the Vatican. It is likewise Monsignor Tardini's department which deals with the problems, often of great delicacy, having to do with the nomination of bishops. Moreover, the first section conducts the negotiations leading up to specific agreements with other States; notably concordats. This accounts for one of Monsignor Tardini's most important achievements, the conclusion of a concordat with Spain.

The groundwork of that agreement had been long years in preparation, but the sweeping demands put forward by the State Secretariat were repeatedly rejected not only by General Franco but by a section of the Spanish episcopate, which was opposed to the tightening of the bonds between itself and the central administration of the Church.

As one calls to mind the crowd of functionaries swarming in the ministerial bureaus of every temporal State, one beholds with astonishment this little group of priests working away in a few rooms of an old Roman palace, where they deal with the complex problems of the world at large. The State Secretariat is now provided with the latest model typewriters. Its telegrams in code go off with the greatest speed and its radio-telephone facilities are on a par with those of any ministry in the world; but over the third floor of the Apostolic Palace there reigns a quiet, even a homelike atmosphere. No such thing as rigid departmentalization exists, with hard-and-fast "channels of procedure" and a bristling horde of functionaries jealous of their prerogatives. The work is portioned out according to the pressures of the moment and the special aptitudes of every person; and it is not at all unusual for some high official to be called upon to write routine letters, simply because he happens to be well grounded in English or Spanish and the letters ought to be written in one of those tongues.

Internal Affairs (the second section, over which Monsignor Montini presided, and in whose stead Monsignor Dell'Acqua now presides) has, for reasons which will appear in a moment, a much larger staff; and it has trebled its force during the past few years. Efforts toward internationalization of the Vatican bureaucracy have there borne some fruit. Frenchmen, Spaniards, North Americans, Germans, and Irishmen are to be found among the personnel. Internal Affairs attends primarily to matters of routine administration, takes up with foreign emissaries questions that do not involve decisions of policy, and carries on a voluminous correspondence with heads of dioceses, superiors of orders, Catholic lay leaders, and so forth.

Little by little, the work of the second section is encroaching upon that of the Pope's private-secretarial staff. Catholics address themselves to the Pope for the widest possible variety of reasons. A nun in the depths of Canada is observing the fiftieth anniversary of her entry into religion and begs the Sovereign Pontiff for a personal benediction. A business magnate wishes to make a substantial gift to the Holy See. A priest has a grave question concerning his ministry which he desires to take up with the Pope in person. French Catholics are forming an association to present the Vatican with a television transmitter. There is no end to the reasons for which people write personally to the Pope. . . . But nowadays it is always the State Secretariat that answers.

Monsignor Dell'Acqua and his staff members also are charged with certain special tasks over which, although these bear only indirectly upon the conduct of foreign affairs, the Pope nevertheless has retained control. One of the second section's latest assignments, for example, is the creation of a Pius XII Foundation, designed to raise funds throughout the world for the financing of the international organization of the Lay Apostolate.

Thus, while the first section deals with affairs of greater importance, the second takes more frequent action and upon a wider front; and Monsignor Dell'Acqua especially is almost always called upon to draft the Sovereign Pontiff's decisions when those are not embodied in a formal text put forth by the Pope himself.

As for the Congregation of External Affairs, which i' an assembly of cardinals and normally supervises the State Secretariat, its meetings are few and far between In theory, such meetings are held to discuss thorny ques tions which have been submitted to the section for External Affairs—pending final decision by the Pope.

XII

The Vatican's World View

FROM THE HALL THAT gives access to the State Secretariat you have before you, through the great window-embrasures, one of the most extraordinary views in the world.

At your feet lies an expanse of St. Peter's Square, with

one of the two fountains jetting its foamy plume against
the blue, and an arm of Bernini's colonnade in gray and
weathered marble. In the background, beyond the ancient
Tiber, stretch the tiles and sun-baked travertine of Rome.
And in the far distance, crest beyond crest in ever
deeper tones of mauve, rise the hills. Even within the
Apostolic Palace walls you can hear the lazy murmuring
of the Eternal City.

On the farther side of the square courtyard are the
blank windows of the Pope's apartment. On that side all
is cool and shady. On this, the sun strikes fiercely in
through faded draperies. The pontifical gendarme, leaning
upon his sword, is nodding off. The wall behind us is
paneled with huge frescoed allegories and inscribed all
over with Latin names.

A glazed door admits us to the outer waiting room.
There we find ushers in black frock coats. Enthroned
behind telephones, they are carrying on loud conversations without visible concern for the bishops and ambassadors who sit waiting their turns in other rooms that
open off from this anteroom. A great bust of the Pope
Gloriously Reigning, carved in glossy marble, dominates
the room.

Into mysterious regions lead passageways along which
black cassocks go gliding to and fro. Venturing a few
steps farther, you suddenly find yourself in a corridor with
a delightful vaulted ceiling whose recesses were adorned
by Raphael's pupils with arabesques and garlands and
birds of paradise. Through the windows here you may
glimpse Michelangelo's cupola from a novel aspect. Down
at its very base, beneath a medieval archway, you will
discover a bored Swiss Guard all alone with his halberd.

If, however, we are daring enough to penetrate still

farther, no more frescoes or gleaming appointments meet the eye. What we find are tiny rooms with white rough-cast walls, rather like monastic cells, which are occupied by young priests who are tapping typewriters or perusing the report of some nuncio who has returned from a distant continent. Supposedly these are graduates of a pontifical academy which trains the personnel of the Vatican diplomatic corps at Rome. It is staffed by retired nuncios who give courses in diplomatic and Church history, the rudiments of economics and sociology, and protocol. In practice, though, the bureau chiefs carry on the recruiting of functionaries for the State Secretariat by direct negotiation with persons of influence in the Curia, with nuncios, and with foreign bishops visiting the City.

Here on the Vatican Hill, in the narrow space bounded by the dome of St. Peter's and the Sistine Chapel, this huge sunlit corridor and this antechamber gleaming with too much wax and this somewhat frivolous Renaissance hallway and these white cells crudely hacked into the labyrinth of ancient walls form the convolutions of the brain of a whole world. Here, pouring ceaselessly in from all points of the compass, come messengers, letters, telegrams, and emissaries of every sort, official or semi-official, some with pomp and circumstance, but many secretly.

Abruptly, then, you are struck by the realization that Europe is only a tiny province. Hemmed in by a threatening sea of communism, it is lost amid an ocean of whole peoples to whom the very name of Christ means nothing. The problems that most concern us grow shadowy and fade insubstantially away, and we discover that the heart of the matter lies elsewhere.

Here, when Asia or Africa are under discussion, the European point of view no longer holds. China, one of the provinces most recently penetrated by the Church, has a native episcopate and its own body of clergy who are resourceful, steadfast, and have for years been undergoing the trials of martyrdom. New countries struggling to be free are not, from here, regarded as endangering some motherland, uneasy over its prestige and investments. They are viewed instead as lands of fresh opportunity where, perhaps more readily than among exhausted Europeans and materialistic Americans, the Christian message may find its way.

Russia is the great enemy and also the great hope: for in Russia there lives and suffers what is at once the most powerful of dissenting Churches and the one least removed in points of doctrine, dogma, and the Sacraments. The arch-enemy everywhere is communism—the counter-church, shrewd and relentless, that has sworn undying enmity to Rome. In China and Poland, in Albania and Galicia and even in Yugoslavia, it is communism which provides the martyrs of today; and at all points, and according to the same strict plan, it proceeds with its efforts to seduce, subvert, debase, or crush the Christian Churches.

Going beyond the mere letter of the reports that are received here, the reading of them yields a unique evaluation of the strength and abilities of men. Events, viewed *sub specie æternitatis,* are appraised according to a peculiar technique, which is the touchstone of sanctity. Politics are regarded not at all as questions of the duration of a ministry or a legislature but in the light of what is held to be the trend of an evolving century or even an era. Historical personages who for us have become no more than disembodied names or figures in a waxworks here retain the very odor of their humanity. From the vantage point of two thousand years, what does the century and a half between Hitler and Napoleon amount to? The Emperor of the French is here no figment around which to spin the poems of a Victor Hugo or a film in technicolor. He is that prince who had the impudence to browbeat a predecessor of the reigning Pope, and the scent of his trail still is hot in the archives of the State Secretariat.

And as for the odor of sanctity, you may find it clinging to the scribbled messages that find their way here secretly; the frequent scrawls that tell of such-and-such a priest burned alive, of so-and-so many others who have been shot or have died under deportation, of the devout who are suffering for their faith. Somewhere, always, the active and bloody persecution of the Church goes on and on. Here the latest news on that score finds its way through the same channels as the item about a reception held by the Nuncio at Madrid for General Franco. All are docketed and filed away with equal care; and martyred priests and Christian populations debauched by violence will duly take their place in the great tableau of the Church Universal and of its destiny, which here is being accomplished without heat of passion or of haste.

XIII

The Vatican and Politics

DOES ALL THIS ADD UP TO
an assertion that the two sections of the State Secretariat
concern themselves solely with Church problems? Not at
all. The times in which we live permit no such separation
between spheres of action, such division into air-tight

compartments. The third floor of the Vatican is too closely bound up with the world at large to allow of its avoiding the swirls and changes of politics. Furthermore, recollections of the temporal power of the Popes are still too fresh to preclude some ambition to play a part and exert an influence. The Secretariat nevertheless has its special point of view. Its main concern—the sole "line" of this Ministry of Foreign Affairs—is the Church's interest. The judgments it forms concerning political developments and parties and party men depend directly upon the usefulness or dangers they present in respect of the Catholic position. Those are the considerations that rouse its sympathy or mistrust, that move it to conclude alliances, propose an exchange of good offices or, contrariwise, set itself in opposition.

However, in such a department, directed as it is by a prince holding absolute powers, personal preferences as well as social ascendancy are bound to enter. Even though the Head of the Church is, by the very nature of his functions, placed above national distinctions and the great game of politics, the chief diplomat of the Vatican— and in the last analysis that always means the Pope—has his sphere somewhat below the realm of the absolute. No inflexible doctrine prescribes the course of his actions from day to day, nor is that course attended by any infallibility. In its contacts with the temporal world, the State Secretariat trims its actions in accord with the temperament of Popes, the fitness of its personnel, and the accuracy of the information it receives. The Vatican endeavors from its hilltop to gauge the temper of the times and estimate what are the main political or economic trends. In this it fares well or ill, depending upon circumstances.

Do its actions and influence amount to a great deal? One must immediately draw a basic distinction. Viewed as a political institution, the Vatican is one thing and the various world-wide episcopates, clergy groups, and laymen for Catholic Action are something else entirely. The different national Churches and local clergy have their own traditions, tendencies, sympathies, and above all their own politics. They are more or less tied in or more or less at odds with the political forces of their respective lands. It is for them to draw up, each on its own account, the list of actions to undertake and perils to avoid, and assign to these a scale of relative importance. They have their own special interests to protect; and in order to do so, they may be republicans in one place and monarchists in another.

It is not easy for the State Secretariat to run counter to such local conditions and to influence bishops or priests according to its own judgment of what is opportune. The nuncios, who in theory serve as liaison between the Secretariat and the national hierarchies, can exercise a considerable influence, it is true; but nowadays they too are in great measure victims of the decline that has been suffered by the forces of diplomacy throughout the world. Outside their sphere of action the great course of world events goes sweeping by, and personal contacts now form too quickly for the nuncios to keep abreast of the trend. Men everywhere, believers and non-believers alike, grow ever more impatient of such political and economic positions as the Church is able to espouse. There never has been a time when the word "clericalism" stood in worse repute.

Unless the problems at issue are purely religious, the Church is by no means always effective in working

directly upon the great body of Catholics. The wide
variety and contradictory aims of the numerous Catholic
parties that may be found all taking part at once in the
politics of a single country will serve to show how impossible it is for a political or economic realignment to
occur in obedience to a summons in the name of religion.
Nor can one adduce the slightest evidence to show that
the Vatican exercised any preponderating influence during the terrible drama of the two world wars. Its presence
carries little weight in international organizations. Its
rôle in the United Nations has been, to say the least,
unobtrusive, with the possible exception of some little
part which its profound hold upon certain Catholic lands,
such as some countries of South America, has enabled it
to play.

Moreover, this divergency of views in matters temporal extends into the ranks of the clergy themselves.
Seldom has there been an era when so much freedom has
obtained within certain of the religious orders in regard
to politics. The Dominicans number among their leaders
men who stand at the extreme Left and at the far Right,
some who are die-hard conservatives and others who are
leftist agitators. Surprising though it may seem, the same
holds true of the Jesuits, whose internal solidarity long
has been a byword.

In short, the situation almost everywhere is too complex and fluid for a clear picture of it to be formed at the
Vatican. Sometimes the men of the Curia miss the correct
interpretation of events in a particular country despite
the fact that they are informed down to the last detail.

When, however, the vital interests of the Church are
at stake, it is a different story altogether. This happens
only when the jealously guarded repository of Faith and

Doctrine is endangered. And that occurs whenever an
attack upon the Church is accompanied by an ideological
war; when a counter-religion to Catholicism is established
and an anti-church is set up. Then it is not only the third
floor of the Vatican that goes into action. The Head of
the Church himself mobilizes his whole government with
the Holy Office in the van, and the action he then takes
will have repercussions in the consciences of Catholics
everywhere. Such, for instance, was the effect of the Encyclical issued by Pius XI against the racialism and
national socialism of Hitler.

There is a third section of the State Secretariat but its
importance today is negligible. It is called the Chancellery of Briefs. There a small staff busies itself with the
drawing-up of *breve,* which are official documents drafted
or countersigned by the State Secretariat. Latin is the
official language and there always are prelates at the
Vatican who are humanistic men of letters. Another
office, under the Curia, the Secretariat of Briefs to Princes,
concerns itself with "Latin letters" in the sense that it is
responsible for safeguarding the sound usage of the language itself, and for adapting the Roman tongue as far as
possible to the demands of modern times. These branches
of the service, in sum, attend to the drawing-up of the
numerous documents that are published in Latin; letters,
written on parchment and sealed with the Fisherman's
ring, which the Pope dispatches to princes; letters on
ordinary paper addressed by him to civil or ecclesiastical
dignitaries, and pastoral letters sent to the devout.

In order to bring the Latin vocabulary up to date,

Monsignor Bacci, head of the Secretariat of Briefs to Princes, has compiled a lengthy dictionary wherein one may find the language of Cicero playing host to present-day terms. Thus, it is Monsignor Bacci's suggestion that the noun "lift" be rendered *cellula cansoria* or *anabathrum*. The word "torpedo" is translated as *aerovehiculum ad infringendas naves*, "airplane" as *velivolum*, "noodle" as *farina subacta*, "telephone" as *telephonium*, "gratuity" or "tip" as *corollarium*, and "pistol" as *manuballistula* or *pyroballistula, ad lib.*

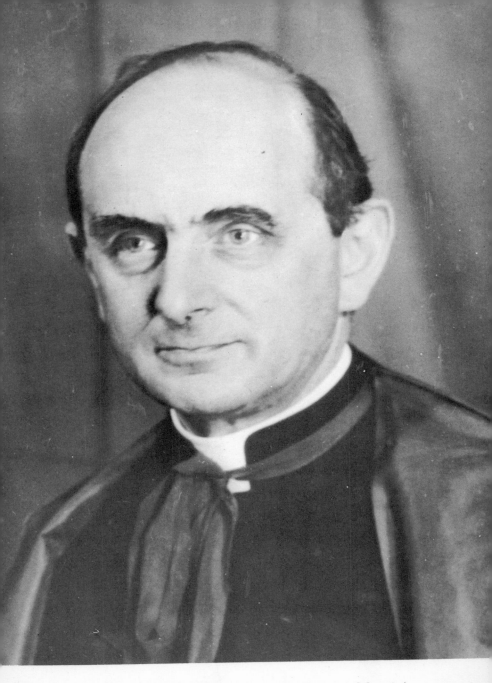

The Most Reverend Monsignor Giovanni Battista Montini

Cardinal Nicola Canali

Part Four

THE CURIA

XIV

The Vatican Bureaucracy

THE HANDS OF THE GREAT clock in the courtyard of St. Damasus, in the heart of the Vatican, mark one-thirty. The gendarme straightens his huge busby. The lifts of the State Secretariat start to creak and groan and in the twinkling of an eye the courtyard, passages, and marble stairways are swarming with black cassocks, accented here and there by majestic violet robes. All, all are hurrying toward the same objectives: a plate of steaming spaghetti, to be followed by the siesta of the Mediterranean lands. At the same hour, the same spectacle may be seen in the vast Palace of St. Calixtus where several of the Sacred Congregations have their offices; in the murmurous lobbies of the Congregation of the Eastern Church; behind the private doors of the Holy Office; at the "Propaganda," which is missionary headquarters; at the Apostolic Chancellery; at the Sacred Penitentiary, and all the extra-territorial palaces belonging to the Vatican throughout Rome.

At one-thirty the clerical bureaucracy of the Roman Curia quits for the day.

In the crowd of priests who suddenly overrun the streets of the Vatican and the palaces of the Holy See there are plain clerics and *monsignori* and monks assigned by their orders to the service of the central Administration. Unless a man is more than commonly unassuming, after some years of faithful service in Rome he becomes a *monsignore* almost automatically; supposing him, that is, to be of the secular clergy, for members of the monastic orders renounce all worldly honors when they take their vows. When a man becomes *monsignore* he exchanges the black rabat that tucks beneath his Roman collar for a violet one. The title *monsignore* is susceptible of a whole scale of gradations, each corresponding to the duties, more or less honorific, that he is supposed to perform at the Papal Court. And those gradations have their reflection in the varying shades of violet of the hose, buttons, trimming, and capes to be worn at solemn ceremonials and official receptions. Purple stands for the highest honor of all (white being reserved for the Pope), and as a man ascends the scale his vestments change from pale lavender to wine-red to crimson.

There are nearly a thousand ecclesiastical functionaries in the Roman Curia not counting the higher dignitaries, the cardinals, archbishops, and bishops who supervise the Congregations. Lay employees serve as councillors and expert consultants or fill inferior positions. The grand total really is quite low when one considers that not only is this an administrative establishment whose territory is the whole world, but that it takes in the kingdom of souls as well.

Stringent regulations issued by Pope Pius XII in 1951 prescribe the manner of recruiting the members of the Curia and lay down rules for their conduct. There it appears that the ranking prelates and chief dignitaries are designated by the Sovereign Pontiff and that notice of such appointments is given by a *biglietto* of the State Secretariat. Functionaries of the middling grade are appointed, as a rule, by personal arrangement between the head of the Congregation and some diocesan or superior of an order. All appointees must be between the ages of twenty-four and thirty-five and not under obligation for military service, come of a respectable and religious family, and furnish a clean bill of religious, moral, and civil conduct. All who are ecclesiastics should in theory hold degrees both in theology and canon law, speak two modern languages, and have a ready command of Latin.

Article 12 of the regulations prescribes that every member of the Curia personnel shall take the following oath: "In the name of Our Lord, I *N.N.* do agree, promise, and swear to be at all times obedient to Blessed Peter and to Our Lord Pope *N.* and his lawful successors; to perform diligently the tasks that may be entrusted to me by this Congregation; and religiously to guard professional secrets. I promise also that I will accept no gratuities, not even in the form of gifts. So help me God and likewise the Holy Gospels, upon which I place my hand."

The subsequent article further requires ecclesiastics to make the Profession of Faith and swear to the oath against modernism (a religious heresy).

The regulations, which were drawn up by Cardinal Canali, minutely cover all possible contingencies and have as their main purpose the safeguarding of top-level authority. Thus they provide, for instance, that on the rare occasions when appointments to the personnel are made on a competitive basis, the presiding cardinal of the Congregation shall be sole judge of who is eligible to compete. It is further stipulated that staff members of a Congregation shall at all times hold themselves at the disposal of their superiors, without claim to special remuneration, as substitutes for colleagues who are absent. Article 40 lays down a long list of prohibitions. It is forbidden for members of the Curia personnel to converse during office hours, to receive callers, to leave the room even briefly without permission from above, to receive gratuities or presents of goods or commissions, or be registered in political parties or associated with groups or institutions not in accord with the doctrine and discipline of the Church. In respect of those who have the benefit of quarters inside Vatican City, it is further stipulated that they must hold themselves on call to report for immediate duty at no matter what hour of day or night, and that they must if necessary work overtime. Failure to fulfill these conditions may, at the discretion of the authorities, result in loss of residence privileges.

There is a wide variety of causes for dismissal. Staff members will be discharged if they betray professional secrets, if they contract debts or commit indiscretions prejudicial to the good name of the Congregation, or if they have to stand trial, even though they receive a verdict of acquittal.

Salaries of the Curia personnel are extremely low. A beginner's pay in 1954 was only $70 per month, with $140 as top for the medium grade; and the most that can be earned at the peak of the career is a monthly stipend of $262.50, which at that is nearly as much as the *Cardinale-Prefetto* of a Congregation draws down. Ecclesiastics receive slightly higher pay than lay employees of the same level because, although the priests often have dependent relatives, they do not as a rule rate family allotments, and also because the clergy are the sole *bona fide* functionaries of the Curia, laymen being employed only on sufferance.

There is no possibility of forming a union or of collective bargaining. The slightest move in that direction, one hardly need say, would be quashed out of hand by exercise of the discretionary power of the superiors. Employees of the Curia have however set up a mutual-benefit association, which became effective in July, 1953.

After thirty-five years of service, employees become eligible for retirement at a pay rate only slightly below their terminal salary, less allotments.

A small group of officials enjoying special privileges are the employees of the Institution for Religious Agencies, which is actually the Vatican bank. The dozen or more specialists who work there have a separate code of regulations and a far higher salary scale than the run of the Curia personnel.

Officials of the Curia as a whole are thus compelled to lead so meager an existence that often it verges on downright poverty. They room in monasteries and procure their supplies from the Vatican City stores, where such products as are available, being exempt from Italian customs and excise duties, are much cheaper than outside. Regulations or no regulations, they frequently tide themselves over until payday by undertaking little jobs out of hours. And all are eligible to fall back upon honorariums for Masses which, for many of them, represent an indispensable source of supplementary income. For, as is well known, devout persons send money from all over the world to have Masses said at Rome in St. Peter's or some other church. Further sums brought to Rome by visiting bishops and other travelers are likewise earmarked for the celebration of Masses. In the office of His Holiness' chamberlain the sums thus collected are placed on deposit, and the Masses to be said, together with the extremely modest fee entailed by each, are evenly divided among the neediest members of the Curia.

Even so, certain ecclesiastics in the Congregations or of the Papal Court find themselves in circumstances often bordering on real distress. In order to escape penury there is one worthy *monsignore* who is compelled to act as guide to the Vatican museums—as an accommodation to friends of friends of his, of course. And the famous composer Lorenzo Perosi, permanent director of the Sistine Chapel Choir, was saved from poverty only by a chance outburst in the Italian press which snowballed to such proportions that it drew the attention of his superiors to what is one of the glories of the Vatican today. Even certain of the cardinals are obliged to lean heavily upon the hospitality of a convent or of secular friends.

The Vatican bureaucracy keeps the wheels of the Church's central offices turning, handles the huge bulk of incoming mail from every country in the world, and catalogues and annotates the archives. "Out of sight, out of mind" is not true of the Church—nor has it been for two thousand years. Accessible files covering the past ten centuries in the archives of the Apostolic Chancellery alone amount to over five thousand volumes of documents. Other collections in that same Chancellery carry the documentation back to the year 238.

You will also find officials of the Curia at tribunals, where they record the procedure and draw up the verdicts. The anonymous army of the Roman bureaucrats has, therefore, the Church Administration in its grip. It rubber-stamps and red-tapes everything from canonizations to excommunications, from the nominations of bishops to clearances approving the rule of some new religious order, from a purchase of real estate by the Holy See to delicate transactions with the other Christian Churches. The whole day-to-day business of the Church throughout the world passes through the hands of the *monsignori* of the Curia. Impotent to make decisions though they may be, these priestly cohorts are not the less powerful on that account. They form the climate of opinion, the imponderable atmosphere of Rome. Patiently, they bring the public sentiment of the capital to a focus; and they manage, often quite unconsciously, to influence the great personages, the cardinals and chief dignitaries, whose formidable opponents or partisans they become. And the pressure they exert upon the Old Man at the summit is formidable.

XV

Questions of Nationality

EVERY SO OFTEN, EFFORTS are made to reform the system. Pius X modernized and reorganized the services throughout. Even more sweeping changes in this area were predicted of Pius XII; but it would appear that the Reigning Pontiff, overworked as he is and deprived (albeit willingly) of a Secretary of State and engrossed in other tasks, has given up whatever intentions he may have had of tackling the problems of the Curia.

The Pope has tried to internationalize the administrative personnel of the Church, however, and the process does proceed apace in certain of the services, notably the State Secretariat. But the vast majority of officials of the central Administration are Italians. What is more, such ecclesiastics from abroad as gain appointment often are broken in by long years of study in the academies and seminaries of the Eternal City, and by the time they have risen to positions of importance they give the impression of being as thoroughly "Romanized" as the native sons.

This preponderance of Italian officialdom has not the slightest effect upon the essential character of the Church, any more than the Pope's national origin alters the supreme functions of his office one iota. It has however become traditional (though at any time the division of electoral ballots can break with this) for him to be an Italian; a tradition which seems logical enough when you consider that the Pope is Bishop of Rome and that Rome is an Italian city, and more sensible still when you picture in your mind's eye the rivalries to which every Papal election would give rise if any national advantage whatsoever were permitted to accrue from the choosing of a Sovereign Pontiff. Sustained by the universality of the problems that press relentlessly in upon the Vatican, the Pope ceases to be of any nationality when what is at stake is the welfare of the whole Church. He becomes then the guardian of her Doctrine, and that Doctrine itself protects and safeguards him against all national bias when the articles of faith are at stake.

But it is far otherwise with the understrappers who man the governmental bureaus at Rome. On that level, national enmities and patriotic zeal and political animosities play their petty rôle. Christian charity has its work cut out for it, particularly in these troubled times of ours, if it is to smooth away the angles and salve the bruises.

Recruited from the ranks of a national clergy which in the main is conservative in temper and straitlaced in its views, the Italian hard core of the Curia is quick to take alarm at developments beyond the confines of the Roman Campagna. Reports of revolutions, no matter from what quarter, horrify it, and it panics at the news of governments overturned. A great respecter of titles, it observes their niceties as to the manner born; and it dearly loves to revere a royal crown wherever it can find one still in use. And at the least suggestion of reform or of bold initiative, it bristles with the liveliest hostility.

Against this general background of a corps of place-holders tamed by centuries of discipline and routine there stand out, plain for even the most casual observer to see, those individuals who are eager, humble, and above all devoted. For such priests as these, the Curia is no mere administrative bureau like any other, with fixed working hours and a set schedule of promotions. They go to their desks and sit down to their typewriters with an awareness of performing consecrated tasks, no matter how obscure. They are ever mindful that the kingdom they are working to maintain is, in the larger sense, the kingdom of souls and not of this world; that what they are laboring to preserve is only, so to say, the rough outer bark, coarse-grained but indispensable, within which, and transfusing all, the Sacraments sustain the Tree of Life. Although their inner dedication is masked by the decorum of priestly discipline, they go to their daily work as to some sacred rite.

And they are many, these priests and monks who are galled by the lifeless routine that afflicts bureaucracies wherever found; though never is it more painfully felt than by men whose vocation urges them to be up and doing. Wherefore they often seek escape from the dull comfort of desks and filing cabinets, and find release in the exercise of their ministry. The Roman slums, the red-light district, the settlement houses and foundling shelters all have chaplains who are temporary "fugitives" from the offices of the State Secretariat or the Congregation of the Holy Office; men who volunteer their services to organize Boy Scout field days or administer the Last Rites in the hovels of the poor. The tame security of the Congregations is oppressive to them.

XVI

How the Church Administration Works

THE ADMINISTRATIVE WORK
of the Church today is carried on by eleven units, which
are, in the order of their seniority: the Holy Office, the
Consistory, the Congregation of Discipline and the Sacraments, and the Congregations of the Council, the Reli-

gious, De Propaganda Fide, of Rites, Ceremonial, Foreign
Affairs, Seminaries, and Universities, and lastly the Congregation of the Eastern Church.

Each of these is organized along the same lines and
presided over by a Cardinal-Prefect. Exceptions are the
Holy Office, the Consistory, and the Congregation of the
Eastern Church, which are presided over by the Pope in
person. The supervising cardinals assigned to them have
the title of Secretary.

Strictly speaking, the Congregation is a group of
cardinals appointed by the Pope, and theoretically all
final decisions rest with it. But sometimes the Cardinals'
Assemblies are unable to get to the bottom of the questions they are supposed to settle and their deliberations
often are rather inconclusive. At such times they drive the
competent service chiefs to distraction. The Congregation
of Foreign Affairs, in particular, when convened to pass
upon fine-drawn political problems, often creates problems for the cautious diplomats of the State Secretariat.

Plenary sessions of the Congregations of Cardinals are
held at the Vatican with great formality. Ten days prior
to the meeting, every cardinal is handed the docket of
matters which are to be dealt with. Each dossier consists
of a summary, drawn up by an official of the Congregation, of the arguments pro and con; a digest of the main
documents; a list of the questions which need to be
answered, and the consultant's report. The whole is specially printed for the occasion by the Vatican press, whose
members are bound by a solemn oath of silence. One of
the cardinals, called the "ponent," studies up the whole
background of the matter and thus qualifies to serve his
colleagues as chairman.

At the meeting, the chairman states his opinion, the

other cardinals have their say, and the matter is settled by majority vote. The Congregation's decision must then be approved by the Pope, excepting for lesser matters wherein the Cardinal-Prefect is empowered to act as the Sovereign Pontiff's deputy.

In the fuller sense of the word, though, a Congregation is understood to mean the departments of the ministry where the bulk of the work is done. And there it often is the second-in-command, the Secretary or Assessor, who determines the whole issue. His function may be compared to that of a permanent under-secretary in any governmental department whose head has cabinet rank—which is to say that he plays a highly important part, no matter how little-known he may be to the public at large. He represents the factor of permanence; for it is he who works up the background material for the Cardinals' Assemblies and assigns the expert consultants and makes the day-to-day decisions. He has his own scheduled audiences with the Pope—more frequently, sometimes, than does the Cardinal-Prefect of the Congregation himself.

The service bureaus hold their own stated meetings, which may occur as often as twice a week. The chief functionaries of the Congregation then assemble in the cardinal's office. Their panel, which is known as the *Congresso*, has power to act upon certain matters without ever referring them to the Cardinals' Assembly at all. It is in these departmental meetings that the Secretary of the Congregation seeks advice on all hairline decisions.

The proceedings of a Congregation are recorded by *minutanti* (those who write up the minutes). They are assisted by *copiste* and *calligraphi* or *dactylographi*, who redraft most of the documents according to the approved Roman style. Clerks of protocol and archivists sort out

the reports. Accountants ticket the Congregation's findings according to the nominal fees payable to the Holy
See. The head clerk then is responsible for collecting
those fees, and for seeing to it that the documents find
their way into the right hands. And at the bottom of the
barrel, hiding behind the pompous names of *Cursores*
and *Janitores*, are the messengers and doormen.

As for the consultants to a Congregation, they are not,
properly speaking, functionaries at all. Nevertheless, they
play an influential part. They are members of religious
orders who are specialists in some particular field. The
Secretary often calls in several such experts to study a
question, unbeknown to one another. And if in this way
no satisfactory solution can be found for some particularly knotty problem, consultants, who always are theologians or recognized authorities on canon law, are formed
into committees to wrestle with it.

Latin is the official language of the Church but the
customary language of the Curia is Italian.

XVII

The Holy See's Finances

THE CURIA DOES NOT HAVE
a separate budget. Several agencies administer the funds
of the Holy See and there is a bank to clear the numerous
financial transactions of this cosmopolitan community, but
nobody could even begin to assess the monetary value of

the permanent art treasures vested in the Vatican and its
churches and palaces.

The finances of the Holy See are managed in two parts.
One, called the Administration of Ordinary Assets of the
Holy See, is under control of the Cardinals' Commission
headed by Cardinal Canali, which exercises virtually
dictatorial powers. The other, called the Special Administration, manages the capital assets of a billion lire in
property titles and 750 millions in treasury notes that
were turned over by the Italian Government to the Holy
See in 1929, at the time of the final settlement of the
Roman Question and the Pope's relinquishing of the
States Temporal. Pope Pius XI managed these large sums
personally. He pledged himself to hand them on intact to
his successor and he used only the increment to finance
the great public-works project in Vatican City. The capital
stood untouched at his death. Since that time the assets
held by the Vatican have been subject to frequent ups
and downs, and every economic crisis has had its effect
upon the funds of the Holy See. Since, however, the
Vatican has no intention of converting its capital into
liquid assets, it can possess itself in patience until the
period of depression ends—nor is it ever at a loss for
expert advisers.

Pius XII refused to concern himself personally with
finances, and does not interfere in the work of the Special
Administration. Surrounded by a small international
"brain trust," its chief scrupulously administers these substantial sums in a manner at once adroit and highly secret.
His position, which is without parallel anywhere in the
world, is the envy of every banker and Minister of Finance. Enjoying an absolutely free hand, he has no Par-
liament, no Council of Ministers, no Board of Directors

to call him to account. He pays no capital-gains taxes, he can make long-term investments; and no matter in what country he does business, the diplomatic privileges accorded to the Holy See are always helpful in carrying out the transaction. Nuncios, bishops, and Catholic laymen, trooping in from all over the world, serve to keep him posted on every contingent eventuality that may react upon the fluctuations of finance. Nowhere else will you find such freedom of action combined with such far-flung sources of information. As a matter of fact the Special Administration, so called, takes on ever greater importance and is actually the agency through which the capital assets of the Holy See are administered in Italy and abroad. Pounds, dollars, and Swiss francs are the Special Administrator's preferred mediums of exchange. Its deposits are mostly with the Hambros Bank in London, J. P. Morgan & Company in New York, and the Crédit Suisse.

One of the high officials of the Crédit Suisse, M. de Maillardoz, resides at Rome and serves as secretary of the Special Administration.

The Vatican's gold reserves are on deposit with the Federal Reserve Bank of New York and are at the disposition of J. P. Morgan & Company. The Vatican is not to be outdone by other States which hold their treasury funds abroad. Transactions undertaken by the Special Administration on the basis of these gold reserves are always made with a view to swelling the parent fund.

It is not to be inferred that the close tie-up between the Special Administration and the United States is founded on any particular political sympathies. Regardless of their political bearing, these financial ties have their technical reasons for being—not the least of which

is the fact that the Vatican, at the moment when the
funds now managed by the Administration were established, made the greater part of its gold purchases in
America.

As noted above, the Vatican bank is called the Institution for Religious Agencies. It receives the deposits and
carries out all the financial operations, investment of
funds, transfers, and so forth, that are undertaken by
the countless religious communities all over the world
when they have representatives at Rome. The affairs of
this bank are controlled by a Board of Cardinals but its
real director is the secretary, Monsignor De Jorio. The
bank's little staff includes both priests and laymen. Only
citizens of the Vatican, the Roman clergy, and religious
orders may use it. Yet its transactions fan out over a great
many countries on account of the innumerable footholds
established everywhere by the great religious orders. A
tiny handful of Italians have been authorized to open
accounts with the Institution. That is greatly to their
advantage, for it means that they can transfer funds
without going through the slightest formality or submit-
ting to Italian currency controls.

But neither the capital assets nor the financial skill of
the Special Administration are enough to supply the
constantly increasing needs of the Catholic Church, which
receives appeals for help from all over the world. Whence
her constant appeals for contributions from the devout.
All over the world there goes on a sort of voluntary im-
post of taxes which in English is known as Peter's Pence.
A portion of the sums thus received is forwarded by the
bishops to the Holy See. North America, meaning the
United States and Canada, is the most generous donor.

The money collected for Peter's Pence by no means

always finds its way to Rome. In many lands, it is spent as fast as it comes in, in an effort to defray some part of the Church's local expenses. In France, for instance, it goes to pay the clergy who receive no subventions from the government. Many other countries which formerly sent substantial contributions to Rome are unable to do so nowadays, whether for political reasons or on account of local needs. Gifts made to the Holy See under the heading of Peter's Pence are very often transmitted direct to the Pope, the more especially when they are substantial.

Every Congregation leads an independent existence, administratively speaking, and the Cardinal-Prefect draws up his own budget. Certain Congregations are obliged, notwithstanding, to fall back upon sources of income from outside the Vatican in order to finance their activities. The Congregation of the Propaganda, for instance, would be helpless to carry the huge financial burden entailed by aid to Catholic missions throughout the world, except for the fact that it has everywhere established or taken over agencies which collect funds for use in the missionary field.

XVIII

The Holy Office

In FLORENCE, NOT LONG ago, I beheld a most remarkable ceremony. With the Prefect of Police and an Army General standing by, the school children were assembled, in the presence of the town notables and of Signor La Pira, the Mayor, to lay

flowers on a bronze plaque which had been let into the
pavement of the Piazza della Signioria. The plaque com-
memorates the burning on this spot, in 1498, of the body
of the Dominican monk Savonarola, who was condemned
by the Inquisition and executed by the Florentine Municipality. On one side of the Mayor, a Christian-Democrat,
stood the young woman who was Communist Mayor of
Ferrara, Savonarola's birthplace, and on the other a prelate representing the Cardinal-Archbishop of Florence.
The man to whom this oddly assorted group was paying
honor beneath the gaze of the Florentine populace was
an ardent zealot, a visionary reformer who had hoped
to change the city's government and purge the morals of
Florence and the Church. He scathingly rebuked the then
Pontiff, the formidable and corrupt Alexander Borgia.
The Pope excommunicated him. The Municipality hanged
him and gave his body to the flames. Now Italy and the
City of Florence are making amends for all that. A movement is afoot, particularly among the Italian Dominicans,
to institute the process of Savonarola's beatification. And
the Church herself, through the Cardinal-Archbishop's
intermediary, today salutes the man whom, five centuries
ago, she allowed to be put ignominiously to death.

The Inquisition has long since changed its name. Nowadays it is known as the Sacred Congregation of the Holy
Office and it no longer burns people—or, to use the
ancient formula, "turns them over to the secular arm." It
has renounced all intervention in temporal affairs. But
the Holy Office, still retaining its primacy among the
Congregations of the Church, does remain the stern
guardian of things doctrinal. It now concerns itself exclusively with men's minds. It has as its responsibility the
tracking down of deviations from the true doctrine, how-

ever slight; and for all such deviations it pitilessly applies sanctions. The most dreadful of these, in the eyes of the devout, is formal exclusion from the Christian community, or excommunication.

Beneath the arched portal leading into the courtyard of the Holy Office, a Vatican plain-clothes man is working a crossword puzzle. The doorkeeper is gold-braided and severe. He raises canaries and does his best to discourage the countless Roman beggars who come to this stronghold of the Inquisition in search of help. The Commissioner, who is the most formidable member of the Congregation, lives with his two "partners" in a suite of rooms one flight up. Their quarters are a scene from Dominican monastic life transferred intact into a Roman palace: a discreet hallway, odd pieces of well-worn glossy furniture, a crucifix, and on the wall the same banal devotional pictures. On the floor above, however, one finds ostentatious reception rooms and disciplined ushers. In the chamber where the Holy Office deliberates there is a long table of darkened oak, flanked by Renaissance armchairs and laid out with blotting pads and the full panoply of a directors' room. Yet somewhere, hidden deep in the recesses of this palace, are the famous archives of the Holy Office to which no one except members of the Congregation may have access. Nor may even they consult them until they have taken a solemn oath which is far more stringent than the one required of other members of the Curia.

The silence of the Holy Office is the deepest secrecy known to the Church. It is as inviolable as that of the confessional. Anyone who breaks that secrecy, even through inadvertence, by even so much as a sign, is *ipso facto* excommunicated; and the form of excommunication thus incurred is so severe that the Pope alone is able to remove it. Not even the Cardinal Grand Penitentiary has power to do so. Here secrecy amounts to an obsession and the dread of indiscretion reigns supreme. There are no statistics concerning matters looked into by the Congregation. One is forbidden to know its methods of procedure. Everything is secret. Every secret is top secret. And that is as far as the most innocent inquiry ever gets.

The Holy Office wears a dual aspect: it is a tribunal which passes judgment upon men and ideas, and it is a commission which clarifies and interprets points of doctrine. When functioning as a tribunal it possesses all the attributes of a penal court. It rules (though nowadays but seldom) in cases of heresy. It acts as court of appeals upon the rulings of diocesan tribunals, or sits as court of first instance upon offenses committed by ecclesiastics when those misdemeanors are so grave as to lie outside the diocesan tribunal's jurisdiction. Such, for instance, may be the case when there is allegation of improper administration of the Sacraments, especially of Confession.

Occasionally, too, the Holy Office takes jurisdiction over the hearings when the moral standing of a member of the hierarchy is seriously compromised. If the offense is proven, the Holy Office may then hand down any one of a whole graduated scale of penalties as provided by canon law. These range in severity from the imposition of a certain number of prayers and acts of contrition, or perhaps a period of retreat in some religious house, all the way to a man's reduction from Holy Orders. This, for a priest, is the severest of all punishments. He is deprived of his priestly status without losing his priestly character, for with that he remains marked as long as he lives; but he has no right ever again to exercise the functions of his priesthood. (In rare instances, a man's reduction to lay status may be granted without sanctions; but this almost never happens.)

Trials conducted before the Holy Office always take place behind closed doors. The accused may perhaps be summoned to come before his judges; but in many instances he can only present his case by means of counsel, who must be chosen with consent of the court.

However, the Holy Office has as its chief function the keeping of a jealous watch over doctrine, and more especially the detecting of the slightest heresy or deviation. The inviolability of doctrine is at once the Church's chief concern and its whole strength. That is why the oldest governmental department of the Church of Rome is the Congregation in charge of the repository of the Faith, and that is also why it outranks all the rest.

Thus it happens that the Holy Office becomes in effect a sort of secret-police bureau whose assignment is to detect and look into the activities of the enemy within the gates of the Church itself. For this work of investigation it has men who are its trusted sources all over the world. The deepest secrecy surrounds their assignment, which is to keep the Congregation informed about the doctrinal and moral condition of every diocese in the Church. But the Holy Office also understands to perfection how to make use of the hierarchical system by which every individual, whether clerical or lay, is linked "through channels" to the Roman Curia and the Sovereign Pontiff. A parish consists of a pastor and one or more associate priests. The parish priest may be under an archdeacon. Often, the diocese is composed of a number of deaneries. Bishops have archbishops over them; and in their work they are assisted by chapters of canons—not to mention the "regular" clergy, such as the Dominicans, Franciscans, and Jesuits, every member of every one of whose religious communities fits into some niche in a system tightly controlled by the superiors of the order.

Besides all this, there never is any dearth of straitlaced and pious souls who consider it their duty to let the Holy Office know of any doctrinal long-goings or moral short-comings that may happen within their ken. The pastor stands exposed to the full scrutiny of his flock and the most trifling details of his life can hardly escape them. Reports from those sources are numerous and frequently unsigned. The Holy Office is in receipt of them from all corners of the earth and one may hear in ecclesiastical circles an occasional complaint that such tip-offs too readily find credence. Whenever the alarm is sounded about something that would seem to be out of line, the Holy Office can look into it through the bishop of the diocese in question. The bishop has under his command a "vigilance committee" of the local clergy who are assigned to watch over the faith and morals of their compeers.

In really serious cases, the Holy Office can send a commissioner vested with ample powers and traveling incognito. Such an emissary can summon and interrogate whatever persons he may wish, after first binding them to an oath of absolute secrecy.

Taking also into account that the central government of the Church is kept constantly in touch, through the Consistory, with all that goes on in every diocese, and that the Congregation of the Religious supervises the conduct of life within the regular orders, one may conclude that nothing, in the long run, escapes the stern vigilance of the Holy Office. It has representatives, as a matter of fact, in those very Congregations.

To use its own terminology, the consultative body of the Holy Office "qualifies" (i.e., rates) theories that are submitted to it or in regard to which it is alerted by its countless collaborators scattered throughout the world. Doctrinal views thus looked into may be, according to the lexicon of the Holy Office, "imprudent," "dangerous," "not consonant," "offensive to pious ears," and, in extreme instances, heretical.

The Holy Office does not confine itself entirely to condemning works of a tendentious character. Anything having to do with the supernatural, and especially all occult or mystical deviations and irregularities, come under its purview. It concerns itself with spiritualism, magic, and sorcery, and, although the various forms of exorcism by means of which the Church combats the assaults of the Evil One upon the soul are within the province of the Congregation of the Sacraments, the Holy Office deals also to a certain extent with demoniacal possession. And indeed if you were to examine the matter more closely you would be surprised at the volume and diversity of the assorted mystical perversions and deviations flourishing in our time. Southern Italy is a fruitful region for tiny cults which spring up in the marginal ground that lies between the fields of civil and canon law. Prosecution in the courts has lately brought to public notice that the practice of witchcraft is still very much alive in France. Switzerland has its share, and Germany too.

Mystical experiences of every sort are carefully screened

and sifted by the Holy Office. The Church, as is well known, regards all such phenomena with extreme caution. Never does she express an opinion on the authenticity of supernatural events or visions during the lifetime of the recipients or beneficiaries. In Bavaria, Teresa of Konnersreuth has now for many years led the miraculous life of a person marked with the stigmata. And for thirty years so has Father Pio, the Capuchin, while fervent crowds come flocking to his confessional in a South Italian village. There is a stigmatist living in Paris. The Holy Office is fully aware of these men and women, and of the marks they bear and the extraordinary piety and exaltation of their lives. But it gives not the slightest encouragement to the interest and curiosity felt toward them by the devout.

Again, it is the Holy Office that sees to the publishing of the Index of prohibited books. The list is compiled by a special committee which follows up leads that are sent to it from all over the world. Theoretically, everything that is published at all is supposed to be passed upon by the Holy Office. As a practical matter, the committee's attention is focused primarily upon theological works and moral disquisitions written by ecclesiastics; for such authors run a greater risk than do all others of compromising the Church's position. Everything published by a member of the clergy is double-checked, besides, through a system of censorship established in each bishopric; but the Holy Office has a reputation for showing itself more stringent than any mere diocesan.

The "reactions" of the Holy Office are anything but prompt. Not infrequently it launches its bolt at books or authors well after their influence is clearly on the wane. This results largely from the discretion of its advisers, but also perhaps from the fact that the Holy Office, being a fixture at Rome, is somewhat affected by the Italian atmosphere. Some few landmarks of literature, indeed, fail to draw its attention until translation brings them more nearly within its view. Thus it happened that the collected works of André Gide fell under solemn condemnation only a short while after their author was no more: the ban being coincidental with a sort of Gide craze which then was raging in Italian intellectual circles, where fascism had earlier prevented that writer from being known.

The Holy Office, acting as guardian of the true doctrine, exercises functions which are sacred to the police. Therein lie its limitations, which serve to explain and justify its unpopularity. Those functions, to be sure, do need to be performed, for the legitimate and proper expression of Catholic doctrine is continually under attack on all sides. But one should not require of the Holy Office that it exert a vital and positive influence over the minds of men. The Catholic conception of dogma, as truth that is actually lived through spiritual experience and not merely defined in the abstract, is a matter which falls under the supreme jurisdiction of the Pope. The guardian of doctrine, in the plain and definite meaning of that phrase, is in fact the Head of the Church.

XIX

The How and Why of Annulments

THE LEGAL PROCESS OF getting a declaration of nullity of your marriage at Rome will cost you a bare minimum of 300,000 lire. Of this, you will have to allow 170,000 lire, at the most, to fee an advocate assigned you by the Rota; between 40,000 and

50,000 lire for the printing of the records, and close to 60,000 lire for the costs of the tribunal. What this all amounts to is $560 in terms of U.S. currency. But to this you must add, of course, the cost of a trip to Rome, if you can afford it, plus traveling expenses for the witnesses. . . . On the other hand, though, you may get through the whole procedure gratis. Forty per cent of all matrimonial cases reviewed at Rome are undertaken without charge.

Only a declaration of nullity makes it possible for Catholics to break the marriage bond. Yet even this flat statement admits of too broad an inference. For, as everybody knows, the Church recognizes no such thing as divorce, strictly speaking. Marriage, according to the Church's teaching, which is founded upon Christ's injunction, "What therefore God hath joined together, let no man put asunder" (Matthew xix, 6.9), is indissoluble. It is a Sacrament enduring for so long as both parties remain alive. A legal separation of the couple, in clear-cut instances of incompatibility, is as much leeway as the Church will admit. Thus, only one chance is afforded by which you may regain your freedom—and that is, to prove that you have never lost it. You must show that your marriage was improperly performed.

There are, as a matter of fact, many marriages in which all the conditions necessary to render them valid in the eyes of the Church have not been fulfilled. If you suspect that your own union may perhaps be less than perfect, in the sense that it is tainted by some legalistic flaw, you should bring the question before the appropriate tribunal; there is one in every diocese.

Procedure will then be instituted to invalidate or confirm your marriage, and the local tribunal will in due course either declare itself competent to rule in the case or else send the record on to Rome. While the diocesan tribunal of first instance has the matter under advisement, a separate diocesan tribunal is supposed to examine the question independently. Only if both courts bring in the same findings and for like cause will judgment be rendered there and then. After that, however, the "defender of the bond," whose function it is to maintain the argument that the marriage is valid, is in duty bound to appeal the case to a third court. If the appellate court upholds the findings of the other two, the marriage is then declared null and void. But . . . there is, in principle, no such phase of decision as a final judgment, and so the process may begin all over again. (The practice of having the same case come simultaneously before two different courts is a commonplace of ecclesiastical procedure.)

The Church regards marriage as a Sacrament administered not by the priest but by the principals themselves at the moment of pledging their mutual consent. The priest before whom this troth is plighted stands only as a witness in behalf of Jesus Christ, in whose name the union is sealed.

There are certain contingencies which automatically render a marriage invalid. Canon law lists thirteen of them: insufficient age; impotency; the bond of a prior union if the other party to it is still alive; difference of religious faith; ordination to the sub-diaconate; profession of final vows in a religious order; abduction of the intended spouse; crime (which term should here be understood to mean adultery before the fact and compounded by promise to wed, or a prior civil marriage, or murder of preceding spouse, or spouse-murder without adultery but compounded by complicity of the other party who wishes now to wed his or her accomplice); consanguinity; kinship within certain specified degrees; common-law relationship to which an invalidated union or open concubinage gives rise, whereby either party to such carnal association is prohibited from marrying the child or grandchild of the other; spiritual affinity, and legal kinship resulting from adoption, but only in such places where civil law runs to the same effect.

In addition to these circumstantial prohibitions, a marriage may be rendered invalid through improper consent. As already noted, consent is of the essence of the marriage bond. The only valid marriages are those to which both parties have consented in full independence and freedom of action and with precise knowledge of what they were about; and it is within this area that ecclesiastical judges may show themselves either liberal or obdurate. Generally speaking, the liberal attitude would seem to be more prevalent. When brought face to face with the storms that rage in ill-assorted households, ecclesiastical tribunals incline toward a more liberal interpretation of the law's provisos. They try to find out whether perhaps there may not have been ignorance on the part of one or the other, or family pressure, or mental reservation, or pre-determination not to fulfill one of the basic purposes of marriage, which is procreation; or the thousand-and-one other causes that may prejudice or weaken the primary resolve. Not long ago the tribunal of the Rota, which is responsible for passing judgment at Rome in matrimonial cases, became alarmed at the liberality with which nullities were being declared in certain of the dioceses. Thereupon a circular went out from Rome. The number of invalid marriages would appear to be on the increase, regardless.

A declaration of nullity may be procured, too, on

grounds of certain defects in the observance. Although administration of the Sacrament of Marriage is performed by the parties themselves, their troth does have to be plighted before a priest. But not just any priest at all will actually do. Ecclesiastical regulations demand that the vows be witnessed by the priest of the parish, the bishop of the diocese, or their delegates. Along similar lines, breaches of observance may be discovered in some neglect of the prescribed procedure regarding the publication of banns or the other precautionary steps taken by the Church in advance of a wedding. And it is appropriate here to bring up the specific case of a marriage which has been celebrated in due form but not consummated. In principle, such a union is every bit as indissoluble as the average, since the Sacrament inheres in the act of mutual consent. Canon law, however, holds that in the case of an unconsummated union, the Pope can pronounce the marriage invalid. Theologians and authorities in canon law are at odds over the justification of this legal paradox, but nobody questions the Pope's power to act in such instances.

Supposing you should find yourself in such a case, the procedure would be for you to file a plea with your bishop, telling him why the marriage has not been consummated and how you propose to prove your statement. The bishop then notifies the Congregation of the Sacraments at Rome, whereupon he usually is delegated to exercise its powers and institute the procedure. The bishop appoints an instructor to brief the inquiry, an attorney to act in your behalf, and a defender of the bond. Every marriage under dispute is presumed to have been consummated and it is up to the complainant to prove otherwise. As it is not always possible to adduce medical opinion in support, especially in the case of a second marriage, the hearings will take under advisement the testimony of witnesses and receive written documents in evidence.

After scrutinizing the findings of this inquiry, the Congregation of the Sacraments at Rome hands up a recommendation to the Pope, who may in person give the couple back their freedom. But often, if the inquiry leaves it open to inference that any new marriage would come to grief for the same reason, the Congregation enters a caveat. For example, it may grant only one of the parties permission to remarry.

Matrimonial cases coming up for consideration at Rome are routed in three different ways, depending upon the main aspects they present: to the Congregation of the Sacraments, the tribunal of the Rota, or the Holy Office. The latter reserves to itself cases arising from mixed marriages between Catholics and non-Catholics.

The Rota, which was established seven centuries ago, is the oldest of all ecclesiastical tribunals, and is housed in the splendid Palace of the Chancellery. It is presided over by a French prelate, Monsignor Jullien; and there the most drama-packed of testimony unrolls as though muffled in a cloud bank, since virtually all of it is presented only in writing. The attorney for the defense offers a printed presentation: twenty pages, following a set form laid down by the tribunal. Twenty days thereafter, the attorney for the plaintiff publishes his reply: six pages. These often are followed by rebuttals on both sides—and so, for months running sometimes into years, the battle of brochures goes on and on. In extremely rare instances, the Rota authorizes the contending parties and their advocates to appear before the judges and make a *viva voce* clarification in matters of detail.

A short statistical breakdown of the cases upon which it has passed judgment during its preceding session is issued annually by the Rota. Following are the statistics for 1953: out of 171 judgments rendered by the Rota in matrimonial cases, 77 invalidated the marriage and 94 confirmed validity. Twenty-five of the annulled marriages were so declared in consequence of hearings undertaken free of charge by the tribunal, which assumed all court costs and fees for the defense. Forty-three verdicts out of the 94 in confirmation of validity were likewise undertaken free of cost.

There is yet another tribunal which holds sessions at the Curia: the Supreme Tribunal of the Signature, which is made up of ten cardinals. It frequently serves the ecclesiastical tribunals as court of last resort. And now and again, in extremely rare instances it sets aside a sentence passed by the Rota and hears appeals from the judgments of that tribunal.

XX

The Sacred Penitentiary

THE SACRED PENITENTIARY
functions in the realm of the unseen. The judges of that tribunal never know the identity of the accused. Cases always are presented under the cloak of anonymity. Oddly enough, it is the most "down-to-earth" member of all the

Sacred College, Cardinal Canali, involved as he is in the temporal administration of the Holy See, who also heads this tribunal which rules upon matters of conscience.

The Penitentiary grants absolution in cases which are "reserved"; that is, it acts in matters involving sins of extreme gravity which the ordinary father confessor, lacking power to absolve, refers to this court or to the Pope himself. Likewise, it is the Penitentiary which has power to remove sanctions that are automatically incurred by a Catholic through the commission of certain crimes. In the graduated scale of those penalties as provided by canon law, there are four kinds of excommunication "very specially reserved," twelve "specially reserved," and the like. The Penitentiary examines into the causes which have led to the application of such penalties and may remove the sanctions thus incurred. Occasionally, the tribunal passes judgment after the fact upon decisions made by a confessor under exceptional circumstances which have prevented him from consulting Rome before granting absolution—as, for instance, to a dying man. The tribunal concerns itself, however, with extraordinary instances only, and it is seldom indeed that the faults committed by a "moderate" sinner go beyond the ample powers conferred upon every confessor.

All that pertains to the "inner voice" falls beneath the purview of the Penitentiary. That is to say, it holds jurisdiction over questions which, while touching upon the devout conscience, are neither apparent to the world nor operative in the sphere of man's relations with his fellows. The Penitentiary deals only with inward disturbances, with disorders of the soul in its relationship to God. For instance, the Penitentiary can release a person from a vow which he has made in the secrecy of his soul but which he lacks the strength to keep. Or again, it can relieve him of "a burdensome heritage of conditions orally and secretly taken upon his conscience but which he perceives himself incapable of fulfilling without grave harm to himself or his family." The Penitentiary, after looking into the attendant circumstances, can remove the obligation and set his soul at rest.

Every Catholic may have direct recourse to the Penitentiary by writing to "His Eminence the Cardinal Grand Penitentiary, Palazzo del Sant' Ufficio, Roma." Usually, however, it is the confessor who writes. He presents the case under fictitious names. The reply comes in an envelope addressed to the confessor. Enclosed is another envelope sealed with the arms of the Penitentiary and inscribed: "To the confessor chosen by the penitent from among the priests approved by the Ordinary of those parts." The penitent then is free to go to his own confessor or to some other, who in either event will speak to him only through the screen of the confessional. To him the penitent delivers the letter under seal from the Penitentiary—and under seal of the confessional he hears it read to him. In this way, freedom of conscience and the secrecy of the confessional are safeguarded to the very last.

Recourse to the Penitentiary is free of charge. And this tribunal, unlike the rest of the Roman Congregations, is quick to act. "For sincere repentance brooks of no uncertainty, wherefore it is important to act promptly and set the penitent's heart at peace."

XXI

Beatification and the Making of Saints

THIN AND PALE, THE CAN-
dles flicker against the somber background of Michelangelo's "Last Judgment." The Sistine Chapel hums with
a throng of patriarchs and bishops. Drenched with incense, it is no longer the museum where docile tourists

137

are herded through to gawk at the famous frescoes. And along the enormous end wall, their nude bodies all compact of more-than-human vitality, stand forth the damned and the redeemed as Michelangelo conceived them.

Now the processional wends its way toward St. Peter's. Old men with flowing beards are in the line, and men in the prime of life, wearing tall white miters. They are flanked on either hand by a line of beardless youths, each carrying a burning taper, their smooth cheeks freshly pink in the gentle glow. Every member of the processional of dignitaries is thus provided with a young acolyte, who helps him put his miter on and off and clears and rearranges the folds of his cope during genuflections.

Here is the entire Church as represented by patriarchs from the Orient, with their miters round and bejeweled or their klobuks shrouded with black veils, and by the cardinals, the archbishops, and bishops white, yellow, or black, and generals of the religious orders, their homespun habits and bare feet conspicuous amid all this panoply of scarlet silks and velvets.

And now the devout who are packed tight to the very doors have glimpsed the Pope. The shout that goes up is almost like a howl as his throne, swaying to the cadence of the twelve bearers' firm and careful tread, nods past above their heads. Upon the throne is a living statue, its body buried from sight beneath the gold-and-silver-embroidered silken folds. Upon the hands are gauntlets of cloth-of-gold bedecked with sparkling rings. The feet are shod with crimson slippers. The face is ivory-calm and pale as wax. Only the jet-black eyes are warm with animation, outsparkling the burning jewels. Volleys of applause re-echo from pillar to pillar and are muffled somewhere far up in the dome. And above the clamor of the crowd, from a *loggia* high over the entrance portal, ring forth the silver trumpets proclaiming the solemn notes of the Pontifical hymn.

More lights now flood the whole basilica. The Sistine Choir takes up the *"Tu es Petrus,"* and the Pope completes his entry in an atmosphere which is a bewildering blend of triumph, fervor, and humility.

On his head he wears the triple crown. Soon he will exchange it for a white miter, the emblem of spiritual power.

The festive procession halts before the Chapel of the Holy Sacrament and on his knees the Pope adores the Eucharist reserved in the tabernacle. Then, resuming his throne, he repeats the prayers of tierce and receives obeisance from the dignitaries of his suite. The cardinals kiss his hand, the bishops and patriarchs his knees, the abbots and penitentiaries his foot.

And now they are vesting him for the Mass. Symbolizing the Church in its entirety, he assumes the vestments and liturgical insignia peculiar to every degree of the ecclesiastical hierarchy. The Pope thus is robed as simple priest and as Bishop of Rome and as Patriarch of the West. Outside it all, he wears a belt of gold which symbolizes his sovereign dignity.

Under Bernini's *baldacchino* the Mass begins. The Pope takes his place upon another throne, which stands in the apse. He is surrounded by cardinals who assist him in the celebration of the sacrifice. The Prince Assistant to the throne stands at his side. On the steps of the throne are seated the Judges of the Rota. In the tribunals that flank the throne are the relatives of the Sovereign Pontiff and Reigning Princes and Chiefs of State and members of the diplomatic corps, all in full uniform or evening dress. And thrice, during the course of the Mass, the Pope ascends to the altar followed by the cardinals and fifteen bishops wearing white miters, and by acolytes too numerous to be counted.

At the Offertory, the cardinals and postulants will approach the Sovereign Pontiff bearing donations: two candles of sixty pounds' weight each, two loaves covered with gold and with silver and stamped with the Reigning Pontiff's crest, two kegs of wine, and three filigreed cages containing a pair of pigeons, a pair of turtledoves, and other small birds.

Such, then, is the solemn liturgy with which the Church does honor to those whom she proclaims to be new-made Saints—and the contrast is striking indeed between the obscure lives of humble mortification, sorrow-laden and often persecuted, through which they have achieved this posthumous glory and set in train the pomp that is on display this morning.

According to Catholic theology, the Beatified and the Saints are the Just who, in Heaven, intercede with God on man's behalf. The Virgin Mary leads this multitude. No one knows how many they are. One of the basic dogmas of the Church is the Communion of Saints, *i.e.* the mutual help that the faithful on earth and the departed can bring to each other through prayer and sacrifice until all obtain everlasting happiness in God.

Only a few of the Elect are "canonized" by the Church.

She then solemnly declares that they are members of the Church Triumphant, and that a public cult and public prayers may be offered to them in order to obtain their intercession with God. A long procedure—which sometimes lasts several centuries—is necessary before this official proclamation is possible. Several degrees must be attained before a "Servant of God" is "beatified," and, after new enquiries into his life, is "canonized" as a Saint.

At the trial of the Beatified, a prelate appears as Devil's Advocate. This expressive title has come to enjoy virtually official acceptance. It means that the prelate is charged with the duty of doing everything possible to prevent a candidate for canonization from becoming a Saint. For the Congregation of Rites institutes a full-dress tribunal, complete with prosecutor and attorney for the defense, with witnesses and judges, to conduct a pitiless and minute examination into the whole existence, both here and in the hereafter, of those who are in process of meriting the honors of canonization.

The calendar of the Sacred Congregation of Rites is crowded with cases of those awaiting canonization. Its *Catalogue of Cases* shows 328 candidacies pending, some of which already date from the fourteenth century. All told, there are 741 such instances awaiting their day in court at Rome. Of those, 64 have to do with individuals or groups who died as martyrs. The inquiry into presentations designed to prove saintliness is painstaking and detailed in the extreme.

One is bound to remark that many more Saints are proclaimed from among the religious than from the ranks of the laity. Is that equivalent to saying that the just are less often to be found among the latter, and that sainthood is more usually the preserve of those who entered into religion here below? Not by any means. This anomaly arises from a much more mundane cause: the procedures of canonization are very costly and long drawn out. What with the operating expenses of the tribunal, and traveling allowances for witnesses, and printing charges for the full dossier, the process comes, on the average, to about sixty thousand dollars. Wherefore, in the case of a lay Saint, it is most difficult to find a family or group that can afford to underwrite so considerable an expense for a procedure which may take decades or even centuries. On the other hand, certain of the religious orders, having all eternity at their disposal, can readily undertake to see the procedure through. And so it comes to pass that among the candidates for canonization there are proletarian Saints who remain paupers still beyond the grave. There patiently they wait, on the wrong side of the barrier, for the day when popular fervor, aroused by sudden prodigies oft resumed, renders their claims imperative and enables them to clear at a single bound the obstacles placed in their way by the circumspection of canon law.

First, the candidacy for canonization of one of the devout who has expired "in the odor of sanctity" is placed before the bishop of the diocese wherein he or she died. The process may be set in motion upon the strength of the continuing remembrance of a spiritual life which was particularly intense, and of miracles attributed to intercession from that source. Next, the bishop of every diocese "wherethrough the servant of God has passed" is called upon to join in the preparation of the case by searching out every slightest trace of the putative candidate's earthly journey through their domains. At the same time, a proctor is appointed at Rome who coordinates the details.

Later on, the Devil's Advocate will be assigned to work with him. If the case in question has to do with someone who lived in our own epoch, the court as thus constituted sends out a summons to all those having first-hand knowledge of the life or good works of the servant of God. The witnesses appear and testify. The interrogation to which they are submitted runs to between two and three hundred questions.

The records assembled by the diocesan court are forwarded to Rome. The Congregation must then decide whether an "apostolic trial" can be held. To that end, a solicitor assigned by the Congregation begins by drawing up a written summary of the dossier. The Proponent of the Faith (the Devil's Advocate) files his objections, always in writing. The solicitor replies. The sum total of these documents now goes into type, and the dossier is printed up as an octavo volume of over one thousand pages. The whole of an earthly existence, down to the remotest nooks and crannies of its physical, emotional, and spiritual life, is therein laid bare and fully documented.

Once the case is opened, a new line of inquiry is begun. Did the candidate carry the practice of the Christian virtues to the point of heroism? If the findings are in the affirmative, the Pope, by means of a proclamation posted upon the walls of Rome, announces the "heroicity" (*i.e.*, heroism plus authenticity) "of the virtues of the servant of God." It is a decisive step along the way to canonization. But ahead still lies the minute examination, to be undertaken by a rigorous board of prelates and physicians, into the miracles and cures attributed to the Saint-to-be. The Church requires manifestations of a supernatural character, for testimonials from purely human sources will not suffice: they are liable to error and weakness. Two miracles are needed for beatification, and a further two, performed subsequently, for canonization. Whereupon, in the Basilica of St. Peter or in the midst of the great square before the same, there follows the flamboyant proclamation of the new Saint.

Part Five

THE CARDINALS

XXII

What It Costs To Receive the Hat

"To THE PRIVATE SWEEP-ers to His Holiness, Your Eminence, one gave thirty-five lire in 1936. Your Eminence may do as he sees fit, but certainly the cost of living has greatly risen since then."

In a tastefully printed-up leaflet, a functionary of the

Sacred Congregation of the Ceremonial thus outlines for a new cardinal the list of gratuities and tips he will have to shower about him by way of celebrating his entry into the Sacred College. He already has parted with a lump sum of 100,000 lire as down payment upon the cost of his funeral. The Curia, ever provident, does not intend to be embarrassed by any unforeseen expense.

It has been some time since the agencies in charge of ceremonial drew up the current schedule of "emoluments and tips" to be given to the Pontifical Household (by which is meant all dignitaries of the Papal Court), the personnel of the Congregations, the State Secretariat, and so on down the line. The listing of such gratuities fills three pages and runs to seventy separate items. Disbursements are to be made in three stages: at the moment of one's elevation to the Sacred Purple of the cardinalate, upon one's receiving the hat, and at the time of one's formal induction as cardinal.

First, the cardinal must contribute some thousands of lire to the Congregation De Propaganda Fide, whose long-standing privilege it is to provide him with his ring. Monsignor Sacristan is entitled, as of 1936, to 165 lire. Item, to the priest, deacon, and sub-deacon of the Pontifical Chapel, 60 lire. To the Secretary of the Sacred College, 270 lire. To the supernumerary masters of ceremony, ditto. To the captain of the apostolic equerries (who are comparable to footmen), 60 lire. To the Accountant of the Sacred College, 270 lire. To the private sweepers to His Holiness, 35 lire. To the grooms of His Holiness' Bedchamber, 25 lire. To the grooms and bearers of the *sedia*, 162 lire. To the verger of the Pontifical Chapel for handing out the books, 30 lire.

A little later on, when the new cardinal receives the

hat, he must give another series of tips to the private
secretaries of His Holiness, to the *valets de chambre* of
His Holiness, to the messenger who delivers the hat to
the house of His Eminence, to the assistant sacristan, to
the assistants of the assistant sacristan, to the private
sweepers to His Holiness (again), to the head coachman
of the Pontifical Household, to the Swiss Guards, to the
bugle-and-drum corps of the guards palatine, to the Vatican firemen, to . . .

And lastly, when the new cardinal takes possession of
the church assigned to him at Rome, he will have to
dispense fresh proofs of his generosity to a specified
number of persons, but more particularly to the minor
employees of the Congregations to which he will belong.

And now he is faced by chores of protocol. For the
cardinal figures, in the order of precedence, immediately
after reigning sovereigns, Chiefs of State, and royal heirs-
apparent; wherefore he must write a certain number of
letters to apprise them of his new rank. Above all, there
should be a special message addressed to Catholic sovereigns. Altered circumstances, however, have in late years
so reduced their numbers that only the King of the Bel-
gians, I believe, now remains to receive this formal
missive.

Next, the cardinal should write to the Holy Father;
and the prefect of ceremonies does not neglect to advise
him of the approved phrases with which the letter should
open and close. The new Prince of the Church will use
the greeting, "Most Holy Father," and will close with:
"I kiss the most holy feet, and I implore the paternal
benediction of Your Holiness." As for letters of dutiful
respect to the Dean of the Sacred College, they should
conclude as follows: "I humbly kiss the hands of Your

Eminence and I am your most humble, most devoted, and very true servant."

In addition to these financial and epistolary obligations, the new cardinal will have to procure his wardrobe, and this is no trifling matter—unless perchance he has the good fortune, as did Monsignor Feltin when he became Archbishop of Paris, to find the robes and vestments of his predecessor in the vestry cupboard, and to be of about the same build.

Pius XII, carrying out to the most minute details his effort to simplify and "democratize" the Curia, has lately put forth a *motu proprio* concerning the attire of cardinals. "We know," writes the Pope, "that the cardinals' style of living already is far removed from the luxurious and that they have the praiseworthy custom of contributing to the support of generous and helpful works the economic means that are placed at their disposal by the patrimony of the Church, the piety of the devout, and sometimes their family fortunes." To make this laudable practice easier for them, the Pope contributes several modifications to the complicated wardrobe of members of the Sacred College; and as an austerity measure he has decreed:

1. That the train be cut from the red or violet cassock.
2. That the train of the *cappa,* which no longer shall be worn ungirt in Papal chapels and during Consistory, be shortened by half.
3. That violet habits (worn during Lent and other penitential seasons) shall henceforth be of wool not silk. However, adds the Pope, "Cardinals who already have procured red habits of watered silk may make use of those on days prescribed by the Ceremonial."

In spite of the Pope's *motu proprio,* the outfitting that must precede elevation to the Sacred College represents no slight expenditure. One of the best ecclesiastical costumers in the neighborhood of the Pantheon supplies the following estimate:

Cassock and mantlet of moire, purple, with silk trim and facings: 120,000 lire ($210).

The same in pure wool: 100,000 lire. (This item was priced after the Sovereign Pontiff's revisions. If it were necessary to make the train of customary length, it would come to 10,000 lire more: saving, $17.50.) Great cloak for street wear in pure wool, purple, with silk revers, velvet collar, gold passementerie: 90,000 lire. The same cloak in violet (for penitential seasons): 90,000 lire. Cape of red silk moiré: 60,000 lire. The same in violet: 60,000 lire. *Cappa magna* in purple moire with train: 85,000 lire. The same in violet: 85,000 lire. Lining of rabbit fur (rabbit serves instead of ermine) to wear under the cloak: 25,000 lire. Belt of purple moire with gold tassels: 23,000 lire. Belt wth silk fringe: 8,000 lire. Mantle of black wool with half sleeves, trimmed in red silk: 42,500 lire.

Following the Sovereign Pontiff's late specifications, it now takes only 31½ yards of red silk to make a *cappa magna,* instead of 33¼ plus 13 yards of violet wool, which is a material saving.

But it never would do to forget the hats. Every cardinal should own at least three: one of red beaver for full dress (25,000 lire), another of black beaver with gold ribands for semi-formal (20,000 lire), and an everyday hat with gold ribands: 8,000 lire. As for the *gallero,* the cardinal's hat that is ceremonially conferred upon the new Prince of the Church, the Pope makes him a present of it.

This summary outline does not take into account the cost of the pectoral cross, the ring, and so forth, for these the cardinal either has before he accedes to his new rank or else receives as testimonials from his friends. Here, though, are the figures for what he will require: a gold cross set with precious stones, about 100,000 lire; a gold chain, 130,000 lire; a gold ring with precious stone, 50,000 lire. A miter, 100,000 lire. A crosier, 100,000 lire.

The wardrobe whose main items I have listed is, as it were, the cardinal's civilian kit. Obviously, he also must have the liturgical vestments appropriate to the religious ceremonies he performs. But those vestments do not appreciably differ from the ones he wore as bishop, for the reason that the cardinalate is solely an outward distinction and has no sacred character at all.

Who, then, are the cardinals? They are the seventy members of the Sacred College. Their number was set by Pope Sixtus V in 1586, and the question often is mooted of increasing it, in view of the fact that the Church has taken in a great deal of new territory since the sixteenth century. The number was fixed by analogy with the seventy Elders whom Moses gathered about him as councillors at Jehovah's command. At the outset, the cardinals were actually the parish priests of the metropolis who waited upon the Archbishop of Rome, or Pope, and served as his advisers. And every member of the Sacred College has to this very day his "titular," a church at Rome, to the end that all Princes of the Church, no matter whence they come, may still be Romans.

To have a church at Rome means, in effect, to be its patron; and to be formally thus installed at the time of the Consistory can prove a great inconvenience to cardinals who are not personally well-to-do. For the church in question, while very beautiful, is all too often so badly in need of restoration that it must at once appeal to its cardinal for emergency repairs. That is why the Pope, when selecting churches for attribution, gives top priority of the most needy to the American cardinals, whose faithful flocks are most liberal in support of good works and most liberally provided with the goods of this world. Cardinal Spellman, for instance, has gained great archeological merit by financing major repairs to his beautiful titular Church of Sts. John and Paul. Out of the seventy cardinals, less than a third are members of the Curia in residence at Rome. Virtually all the rest are diocesans.

The allocation of hats to the various countries of the Catholic world is a vexing problem, for the reason that the oldest nations try hard to retain their positions of ancient privilege within the fold of the Sacred College. The younger nations now are crowding in, while the new countries too are clamoring for the purple. In South America, which always goes hungry, great disappointment and dissatisfaction greet the outcome of every Consistory.

The Consistory is an assembly of all the cardinals who are present at Rome. In the beginning, such meetings were occasions of real debate between the Sovereign Pontiff and the cardinals over important questions of Church government. The Pope's position as absolute sovereign, though, has long been settled beyond dispute and the Sacred College has lost all deliberative powers.

Nowadays, the Consistory is nothing more than an opportunity afforded the Pope for addressing some particularly solemn and often secret message to the highest officials of the Church. It is also during a meeting of the Consistory, whether "secret," "semi-public," or "open," that the Pope announces the creation of new cardinals.

Beatification Ceremony in St. Peter's Basilica

His Eminence, Francis Joseph Cardinal Spellman

XXIII

Domestic Arrangements of a Prince of the Church

THE CARDINAL HAS SENT his car for me. It is a ramshackle limousine, long and black, driven by a youthful monk, Brother Alexis. In I get and we tool away toward our destination, which is a small villa in a fashionable suburb. A benefactor of the

order (for the Cardinal belongs to the "regular" clergy)
underwrote his lease of the house when he received the
hat. The donor also furnished the wherewithal to pay the
tailor for running up the requisite wardrobe. For the
new Prince of the Church was without private means
and the order was too poor to foot any such expenses.

The order did provide the Cardinal with a household
by assigning him several lay brothers: a Brother Chauffeur, a Brother Cook, a Brother Footman, a Brother
Secretary. To meet the demands of etiquette, an elderly
British friend, who chanced to be living at Rome on a
small income, was appointed gentleman-in-waiting. A
pious neighbor's nephew is imported from the country
to serve, upon occasion, as train-bearer to the Cardinal at
high ceremonials.

Brother Alexis turns smartly in and here we are at
the abode of His Eminence. He is a thin old man, very
tall and stoop-shouldered. His sharp profile appears as
though carved out of ivory. Squinting nearsightedly, he
is puzzling over a sheet of paper covered with a tiny
scrawl. As we enter the room, he turns toward me a
childlike gaze of searching candor. Then he smiles, and,
scrabbling through the mass of documents that clutters
his desk, he finds his episcopal ring and slips it on.

"Come, come, my child," he says, extending his hand.
"Kiss this ring—it will earn you indulgences."

Scarcely have we started to converse when we are
interrupted by a discreet knock on the door: "Luncheon
is served."

We pass through two tiny parlors set out with red
armchairs. The round table in the dining room is laid for
five: the Cardinal, Brother Chauffeur, Brother Footman,

Brother Secretary, and myself. We all say the Benedicite
and Brother Cook brings on the spaghetti. It is followed
by zucchini fried in olive oil, a bit of Bel Paese cheese,
and stewed fruit. An excellent Frascati sparkles in a stout
carafe, and with the dessert His Eminence and his guest
each rate a cup of verbena tea. At the close of the meal,
we all say a decade of the rosary in the Cardinal's private
chapel. Whereupon His Eminence sits down at his piano
and favors me with a rendition of "The Maiden's Prayer."

Not every cardinal leads an existence so frugal and
monastic as that of Cardinal Lépicier, upon whom I often
went to call in his latter years. Even so, the financial
situation of the cardinals of the Curia is a frequent cause
of anxiety, for Princes of the Church who are scions of
rich and noble families are few and far between, nowadays. As a rule, the cardinals have nothing to live on
but the stipends that go with the lofty posts they hold.
The Holy See's exchequer provides each cardinal of the
Curia with a sort of civil list which is called *il Piatto*
(the Dish). At the present time *il Piatto* comes to between
three and four million lire per year, or $5,700 on the
average. Cardinals who are heads of Congregations draw
down an additional $262.50 per month, and a slight
increment to this is allotted to such of them as perform
added duties with other Congregations.

The sum of all this is in many instances barely enough
to cover the costs of an establishment upon which protocol imposes numerous obligations.

A cardinal's apartment, according to the specifications
of the Sacred Congregation of the Ceremonial, should
display the following characteristics: a staircase, of tidy
appearance and separate from the service stairs, should

lead to a dwelling composed, apart from the living quarters as such, of a vestibule, a waiting room, a room for committee meetings, a throne room, a reception room, and a room for the private chapel. The door of the vestibule should be canopied with a baldachin lined with red fabric. Within the vestibule, a bench upholstered both seat and back with material of red wool should run the length of one wall; and this too should be surmounted by a baldachin trimmed with a fringe of yellow silk. The cardinal's coat of arms should be centered upon the back. His arms should likewise be displayed upon the doors leading into the waiting room, where should be provided a small hat rack specially reserved to hold the red biretta. The throne room is to be carpeted in purple. Upon the farther wall, a red baldachin with gold fringe shall surmount a portrait of the Pope.

Every cardinal is supposed to have his "family," by which is meant his court. Although this tends to dwindle more and more, it must at the barest minimum be composed of an ecclesiastical chamberlain, a gentleman-in-waiting, a caudatary chaplain (who bears the train), and a head butler or majordomo. Each of these dignitaries must wear a costume prescribed by the Ceremonial. The gentleman-in-waiting, for example, dresses in black-silk knee breeches and silk stockings, shoulder cape of moire, silver-buckled shoes, short sword, and a bicorne with black ostrich plumes.

A commodious automobile with chauffeur is a necessity. The theory is that a cardinal should never traverse the streets of Rome afoot. Princes of the Church occasionally disregard this rule—in which case they are urged to avoid the main thoroughfares.

The difficulties of keeping up such an establishment are so great that most of the cardinals of the Curia live close to the Vatican in apartments belonging to the State, or in the buildings where their Congregations are housed, or in the many extra-territorial palaces belonging to the Holy See. Thus it happens that the Palace of the Holy Office alone houses five cardinals.

The least affluent of the Princes of the Church get along on various contingent resources. All cardinals belonging to the Curia are "patrons" of a great many monastic orders and of some particular sisterhood whose interests they watch out for at Rome. The Pope in person makes these patronal assignments, and in so doing he takes into account the state of the new cardinal's finances. If those are flourishing, the Pope allots him the protectorate of communities which are in want. Contrariwise, should the cardinal be poor, the Pope makes him patron of several prosperous communities which may tactfully come to his assistance, if only to the extent of inviting him to spend his holidays in comfort.

An infrequent but most effectual way of bolstering his resources is to send him on a legation. When ceremonials of the highest solemnity are to take place abroad, the Pope sends a Cardinal-Legate, who, as his personal representative, is received with all honors due the Sovereign Pontiff himself. Certain legations have become landmarks in the recent history of the Church because of the fortunate results that have ensued. Most notable were Cardinal Pacelli's legations to Lourdes and to Lisieux. The Latin-American countries, being as devoted to festive occasions as they are Catholic, vie with one another in triumphal receptions for a legate of the Pope. Costly

presents mark the stages of his progress. The Archbishop
of Palermo, Cardinal Ruffini, loves to tell how, during
such a legation, he was invited to luncheon by a well-to-
do family. At dessert, in came a huge cake, and in his
portion the Cardinal-Legate had the happy surprise of
finding a diamond of great price.

XXIV

The Sacred College and the Simple Life

THE TRADITION OF THE
Renaissance cardinals would appear to be completely
reversed. No longer are there any such princely patrons
of the arts and accomplished party-givers, beguiling their
time with affairs of the court. Paul Bourget and Zola and

d'Annunzio, even as late as their own generation, could report the spectacle of purple-clad Princes of the Church majestically stalking along the Appian Way. Golden fell the dying splendor of the sunset along the tawny arches of the aqueducts and upon the roseate tombs, as, at a walking pace, a carriage with liveried coachman and footman followed after an old man swathed in silk. And thus did the cardinals of those days honor the custom forbidding them to stroll the streets of the Eternal City. They kept a stylish turnout and were not timid about allowing themselves to be seen in the brave attire prescribed by their high functions at the Vatican.

Nowadays, you may often run across a Prince of the Church incognito on the sidewalk, right in the middle of the City, his long black gown indistinguishable from the habit of the priests who throng in every street. As I remarked a moment ago, the Pope himself has published a decree curtailing the cardinals' robes with a view to rendering their attire more democratic.

There still are Roman cardinals, however, who maintain a palatial residence in the hills of the Abruzzi or at Frascati; who cultivate the vine and appreciate the refinements of great cuisine. When at Rome, they conform perforce to the austerity that is the order of the day and they lead hard-working lives, interrupted but seldom by attendance at embassy dinners or the soirées held by families of the "clerical" aristocracy. You may catch a glimpse of them behind the blinds of long black limousines. Their majestic bearing they owe, perhaps, to many an observance of stately liturgy and the clouds of incense in the basilicas. Once they set foot in their domains, though, they recapture the full stateliness of the noble lord. Then word of the arrival of the *Eminentissimo* spreads throughout the village as if by magic. First comes the archdeacon or the parish priest bearing gifts of an almost ritual character, and then come the local bigwigs doing likewise. In the vast kitchens of the ancient abode, great fires are kindled in preparation for the feasts to which the Roman friends of His Eminence are bid. And the populace lets slip no occasion that may serve as an excuse to set up triumphal arches for "their" cardinal and cover every wall with hastily printed proclamations in honor of the Benefactor, the Protector, "The One Who Comes in the Name of the Lord." Big marble tablets in the parish church memorialize in flowery phrases the cardinal's generous gifts; and there is not a soul in the village, be he never so good a Communist, who does not hope to see "his" cardinal one day ascend the throne of St. Peter.

But these are the exceptions. The streamlined cardinal of the modern age girdles the globe by plane, like Spellman, or addresses rallies of Communist factory workers, like Lercaro, Archbishop of Bologna, or goes on tours of inspection all over the Middle East, India and the United States, like the Dean of the Sacred College, Tisserant.

There are startling differences of tempo and temperament among the cardinals living far from Rome, nearly all of whom are diocesan chiefs, men often at the spot where combat rages and consequently compelled to work at high pressure in keeping with the ever more feverish pace of modern life, and the cardinals of the Curia, who, in the tiny town which is Vatican City, become set in stodgy small-town ways.

The cardinals of the Curia are gradually shrinking in numbers. As of this writing, there are nineteen of them; and the only one who is not an Italian is the Dean. Born in 1884, he is one of the youngest cardinals resident .t Rome but is the senior in point of nomination. The age of the cardinals of the Curia averages very high, and the Sacred College, taken as a whole, has a long life-expectancy. There are at present twelve cardinals past eighty and twenty-seven who are more than seventy years old.

Cardinals of the Curia are not, as a rule, persons of brilliant attainments. Chance and fortuitous circumstances have played a part in certain of the nominations; but the fact of the matter is that a cardinalate at Rome, for a long while past, has been the fitting conclusion to a meritorious administrative career.

It has been known to happen that cardinals placed at the head of Congregations have grown senile at their posts. That always gives rise to problems all down the line, for nothing at the Vatican is harder to achieve than the introduction of new blood into the system. A strong and sometimes even ruthless assertion of the Pope's authority is required if a Prince of the Church is to be compelled by sovereign decree to step down from a task for which he is no longer fit. Nor is that the worst. Some of the old-timers, not content with working on as heads of Congregations after their powers begin to flag, start adding to their functions. This acts as a brake upon regular promotions and leads to inconveniences which, the temperament of the present Pope being what it is, are allowed to continue in default of drastic decisions.

Part Six

THE FORWARD LOOK

XXV

Trustee of the Eastern Church

As HE MAKES HIS ENtrance into the drawing-room of a Roman palace, Eugène Cardinal Tisserant, Dean of the Sacred College, is a proud and arresting figure. A pair of footmen carrying lighted candlesticks precede him. With his purple

cape slung over his broad shoulders and his chest adorned
with a sparkling jeweled cross, he might be, with his
silver-streaked black beard, a patriarch from a canvas by
Raphael or Titian.

The two lighted candles are required by etiquette, so
bear that in mind when next you receive a Prince of the
Church into your home, and do not neglect to give instructions accordingly to the pair of link boys who stand,
of course, at the foot of your stairs. It is a Rule. Nor must
you ever forget that a cardinal ranks by assimilation with
Princes of the Blood. And just one thing more: remember,
when you are in the presence of Cardinal Tisserant,
that he is the chief personage of the Curia.

Quite apart from his exalted duties in the Sacred College, Cardinal Tisserant holds another post in the Roman
Curia which places him at the very summit of Church
government and gives him powers comparable to those
of the Pope himself. He is Secretary of the Sacred Congregation for the Eastern Church. When speaking of the
Catholic Church, one always has in mind the Latin or
Western. That is erroneous. Catholics of the Latin Rite
form only a portion of the Church, albeit the most
numerous; and it is true that the Eastern Churches, while
in the main preserving the characteristics of their origin,
have broken away from the jurisdiction of Rome and are
therefore in schism. But in the Roman Church the Oriental tradition is of the utmost importance, for to it be-
longed the principal Church Fathers.

A multitude of Christians who follow the Eastern Rite
have remained loyal to Rome: there are communions of
Catholics among the Ruthenians, Rumanians, Armenians,
Copts, Ethiopians, Syrians, Maronites, Chaldeans, and
Malabars. Nearly nine million souls, scattered over all

the world, but distributed for the most part throughout the Near East and Eastern Europe, are Catholics of the non-Latin Rite. All those are under jurisdiction of the Congregation for the Eastern Church. The powers of the cardinal who presides over them are far more extensive than those his colleagues of the Sacred College hold over the Roman Congregations they head. True, the Pope in person has title as Prefect of the Congregation for the Eastern Church. In practice, however, the Secretary who sees to the effective conduct of the work enjoys a position of far greater independence than do the other high officials of the Curia.

Cardinal Tisserant is beyond doubt one of the best informed of living persons about the situation beyond the Iron Curtain. And yet, although by temperament communicative and a fluent conversationalist, he is, on that subject, the least talkative of men. Through the grapevine, he is kept in touch with people under his charge who are spread throughout the Communist countries; with clandestine parishioners and with their priests who have gone underground, or who are in concentration camps. Many colleges and seminaries, in Rome and elsewhere, harbor those who succeed in breaking through the cordon. Contacts are established, too, with the steady stream of refugees who have made their way westward since the war. The people who have broken through the Iron Curtain now number several millions. Besides an emigré press totaling hundreds of newspapers, they have broadcasting stations, universities, and an ecclesiastical hierarchy.

As trustees for the interests of the Eastern Church confided to their supervision, Cardinal Tisserant and his Congregation evaluate the information that comes

through to them; and they are carrying on a planned
course of action, the full scope of which will never be
known until the day when freedom of speech and worship are revived in the Iron-Curtain lands. Paralleling this
action, they are discreetly conducting another course,
which consists of a slow, patient, and steady negotiation
looking toward the reunion of the Eastern Church with
the Church of Rome.

The small waiting room of Cardinal Tisserant's office,
only a few steps from the basilica, puts one in mind of
an old-fashioned country lawyer's. The walls are decorated with pictures of the present head of the Congregation and of the cardinals who preceded him. Up until a
year or so ago, you might have seen here a small easy
chair with embroidered cushions, and a cord strung from
arm to arm to prevent anyone, no matter how eminent,
from sitting in it. That was the armchair of one of the
Saints most recently proclaimed by the Church, Pope
Pius X.

Amid these homely surroundings, whispering together
while they wait, stand several handsome and bearded
prelates. They are wearing outlandish turbans from beneath which their hair descends in a mane upon their
shoulders, and their cassocks are full-draped like bur-
nooses. They fall upon their knees when the door opens,
revealing the Cardinal. His Eminence holds out his hand
for them to kiss his ring. Ceremonious greetings fly back
and forth in Arabic. And all at once, here in this stuffy
ministry in Rome with its dozing ushers, one seems to

catch a sudden breath of the Arabian Nights. For Cardinal Tisserant also exercises supervision over the Arab world, and over Catholic Christians of the Near East in particular. And it well may be to this aptitude that he owes his elevation to the lofty post he holds today.

Born in Nancy in 1884, Eugène Tisserant gave proofs from childhood of a dual vocation. He desired to become a priest and to pursue Biblical studies. In Paris he learned Hebrew, Syriac, Sanskrit, Arabic, and Amharic; and he later mastered Armenian and Russian. Before long, the youthful abbé was teaching Sanskrit in Rome, while at the same time serving as curator of Oriental manuscripts at the Vatican Library. Abbé Tisserant was well embarked upon the austere life of scholarship. He published volumes of Biblical studies, edited several Amharic (*i.e.,* Ethiopian) codices, and became one of the world's outstanding Orientalists. As a relief from his bookish labors, he took a horseback trip from Jerusalem to Bagdad. From Mesopotamia he returned to Palestine—but this time by car, as chief of the First Bureau, General Staff, of the French Expeditionary Force during the First World War.

Following the Armistice, he returned to the Vatican Library. There, after a visit to the United States, he initiated a huge project of modernization. In Rome, sharing his enthusiasm as bibliographer, was a man who for many years had been Curator of the Vatican Library— Pope Pius XI.

And so it came about that the quiet and studious career of Abbé Tisserant was suddenly interrupted. For, without his ever having been a bishop, Pius XI named him Cardinal and put him at the head of the Congregation for the Eastern Church. He was consecrated bishop

by the present Pope, at that time Cardinal Pacelli; and
thus overnight the learned librarian was raised to one of
the highest positions in the government of the Church.

The ranking member of the Sacred College is one of
the best-liked members of the Curia; and that, too,
despite the fact that he is not an Italian. Nor a conformist.
He gets up at five A.M. and says Mass in his apartment
on the Via Po, where his brother and sister-in-law keep
house for him. His devotions performed, the Cardinal
makes his way across Rome to the huge offices of his
Congregation—on foot. At two o'clock he returns home
by car, and after lunch he sits down before his dictaphone
and records, in assorted tongues, his letters, reports, and
pastoral messages. A typist comes to transcribe them
immediately.

Sometimes, as twilight draws in, the Cardinal goes one
flight down and finds himself surrounded by the romping
flock of children belonging to his niece, who is married
to Professor Missonier, of the French Lycée of Rome.
After that, it is back to work again—unless, of course,
the Cardinal has accepted an invitation to be guest of
honor at some gala embassy dinner. Occasionally, too,
a ceremonial in one of Rome's great churches awaits his
presence. He makes his appearance then clad in purple
from head to foot, followed by his gentleman-in-waiting
and his secretary and his train-bearer, and the assembled
clergy receive him with chants and incense at the church
door.

XXVI

West and East

IN THE EYES OF THE
Catholic Church, the importance of Eastern Christendom
is very great, even though practicing observers of the
Eastern Rite in Rome are few in number. Not only does
the Church Universal regard itself as in no sense coter-

minous with the Western Church, but, while maintaining that it possesses in fullest integrity the sum of revealed doctrine, it also is ever conscious of the mutilation it suffered when huge segments of Christendom broke away. The Eastern Church parted from Rome on the sole grounds of dispute over matters of discipline. And today, parallel to the Church of Rome, it leads an existence equally rich in sacramental life and stemming as directly from the Apostolic beginnings of Christianity.

In consequence of a long series of controversies both theological and political (but more especially the latter), the Eastern Churches, including the Russian, refused to recognize the Pope's power as Supreme Head. Thus, in the eyes of Rome, they became schismatics; but no one has ever contended that they have not retained, on a par with the Church of Rome, the full validity of Holy Orders as transmitted from generation to generation by the laying-on of hands, and consequently the sacramental validity of rites administered by the priesthood thus ordained. That is why the deprivation suffered by the Church through the defection of the Orthodox is the most serious of all.

"The Church of Jesus Christ," said Pope Benedict XV, "is Catholic but not Latin, nor is it Greek or Slavic; there is no difference between one and another of its sons."

We have there the reason why the feeble minorities of the non-Latin Rite that remain loyal to the Pope are regarded by the Church as having a value out of all proportion to the number of adherents.

Today's supremacy of the Latin Rite within Catholicism is nothing but an accidental phenomenon. It is an accident, to be sure, which has lasted for nine hundred years;

but, since the Church does not reckon time in terms of
the human span, this looms as no greater than a century.
"The Catholic Church of the future," so writes Father de
Vries, a professor at the Pontifical Oriental Institute,
"ought to embrace the Eastern Churches organically and
with equal rights, just as before the schism, and it thus
is bound to acquire a totality of spiritual configuration
differing from that of the present Church, which before
all else is Latin."

The division of the Roman Empire into Eastern and
Western was doubtless what gave rise to the schism.
Basically, therefore, its motivation was political. Rivalry
between the Latins and the Greeks, and the desire of the
Emperors established in Constantinople to regain their
grasp, according to the ancient tradition of Cæsaropop-
ism, upon temporal and spiritual power both, were the
factors that gradually set up the Patriarch of Constantinople in opposition to the Bishop of Rome, defending
as he did his claim to be the successor of Peter, Prince
of the Apostles. These factors by the same token made
the Patriarch dependent upon the Emperor. Nine hundred
years ago, in 1054, Michael Cerulerios, Patriarch of Constantinople, was excommunicated by the Pope and took
the East into schism. And when, later on, the vast Russian
Empire was converted to Christianity by Byzantium, it
followed the dissident Greeks.

But the differences between the two Churches were not
wholly political, even then. Actually, the Church of the
West and the Church of the Orient stand for two traditions, two different *mystiques,* two interpretations of the
same basic message. In proportion as the heads of the
Eastern Church knuckled under to the temporal power
(and the process still goes on), a Church in the truer

sense, purely inward and contemplative, brought the
devout more closely together. This divorce between the
politicking hierarchy and Christian mysticism did not at
all disturb the vitality and depth of belief. But, as the
Christians of the East took refuge in prayerful solitude,
the feeling that between the life of the world and spiritual
experience there is an essential incompatibility became
basic to their religion. In the West, the Church pursued
more and more the course of practical and direct action.
It cut down on ceremonial, hammered out its Latin form-
ularies, and purposefully launched the armies of the
devout upon the conquest of humanity. It went methodi-
cally about the work of concentrating its forces, of
organizing its hierarchy according to the traditions
handed down by Roman Law. And all this while the
Eastern Church was growing ever more apathetic to the
political activities of its officials.

If labored too hard, such characterizations always are
too arbitrary; and there is no question but that an intense-
ly contemplative life can be found in the West as well.
What matters is that two separate trends have each been
artificially prevented from complementing the other to
form a harmonious whole. If their union should come
about, Christianity could be the bridge between East
and West.

One may visualize how much more ample the life of
the Church would become if the Christians of the East,
augmented now by those of Russia, were to rally once
again to the central government of Rome. The schismatic
communions number today some fifty million souls. Many
of those are undergoing persecution because the majority
are to be found under Communist control. Others are
enclaves within the Arab lands. Upon them devolves the

formidable task of maintaining contact with Islam. Thus, from Russia to Egypt, from Bulgaria to Israel, from Rumania to Syria, and from Persia to Ethiopia, the Church is in possession of bridgeheads and has a number of isolated outposts which still are holding across the centuries.

Nor should one overlook another rôle which the Orthodox can play in the broader problem of Church reunion. Churches of the Eastern Rite, following a scheme which often is more psychological than theological, frequently serve as liaison between the Protestant bodies and Catholicism. Protestants and the Greek Orthodox have in common their mistrust of the Pope. But the Orthodox retain what the Protestants have lost and for which some of them, in England especially, still hanker: the Apostolic tradition and the regular administration of the Sacraments. Ecumenical councils of a sort, where Protestants of every sect and the Eastern Church get together, are frequently organized. The Church of Rome refuses to participate formally in such councils but occasionally it does send observers. At Rome, too, the Jesuit Father Charles Boyer has for some years conducted discreet maneuvers as head of the movement called Unitas.

It has been a long while since the Catholic Church last called an ecumenical council. As of now, the Pope is in sole and magisterial exercise of power. The times are not propitious for an assembly of the bishops and theologians of the Church Universal. Nor is the fact that the whole world is living under a continual threat of political and social upheavals the only reason. It also may well be that the Church feels too weakened through dissidence and schism to be able to effectually bring off such a council with fruitful results. Theology itself seems nowadays to be undergoing a crisis. Professors in the universities and seminaries restrict themselves to a repetition of the same old Thomistic formulations; with the exception, that is, of here and there a free lance who once in a while may try to adapt the elements of contemporary philosophy to the traditional teachings of the Church.

Apparently there is nothing for it but to await the day, problematical at best and certainly remote, when a great Council shall bring together the principal Churches of Christendom—or those, at any rate, that have in varying degrees preserved the greater portion, both Occidental and Oriental, of the Christian heritage.

XXVII

The Church and World Communism

AT THE TIME OF THE 1953 Consistory, one of the most important held in our day, and while Rome itself was all smiles and congratulations, the Vatican's semi-official newspaper, *L'Osservatore Romano,* published in full the notes exchanged between the

Holy See and Yugoslavia prior to the breaking-off of diplomatic relations. Roman prelates and sightseeing pilgrims alike were thus brought rudely down to earth, for the State Secretariat's bill of particulars to the Tito government might well serve as a guide to anti-Catholic tactics in the Communist lands. The Consistory, reverting then to its true character, became more like a council of war and less like a family reunion.

The Sacred College is ever mindful of the absent Cardinals: Mindzenty, the Hungarian, released under surveillance after physical and psychological torture and long imprisonment; Wiszinski, the Pole, still in jail; Stepinac, the Yugoslav, under house arrest.

Archbishops, bishops, and nuns deported from China have described in detail the tragic predicament of Catholics in the territories of Mao Tse-tung. And from Bombay the new Indian Cardinal, Valerio Gracias, reports grave Communist threats to his country.

The Korean War has wiped out all Catholic activity in the North. Priests, missionaries, and parishioners were slaughtered.

At Rome itself, only a few hundred yards from the Vatican, there is the "Red Zone" to give the Pope cause for worry. Put up during the war, it is a city of barracks where nowadays the teeming families of a sub-proletariat doomed to hopeless unemployment eke out a penniless existence. Others, more wretched still, find shelter in the ruins of the Roman aqueducts. Here is a gang ready to the hand of willing shock troopers who are well trained and eager for action. During recent municipal elections, the Christian-Democratic administration has had a hard time staying in office. The chairman of the City Council is a crypto-Communist.

In short, from every side come reports which have put Rome on guard; but especially from the heart of Asia.

In that rainy Roman January of 1953, Monsignor Romier granted me an interview in his glacial room at the International Missions House. He has spent forty years in China, from 1912 to 1953, with only two trips home to see his relatives in France. His face has taken on the semblance of a Chinese mandarin's. He is slant-eyed, and a long straggle of thin beard accentuates the prominence of his high cheek bones. In his speech, the accents of Bordeaux are strongly flavored with suggestions of Russian, English, and Chinese. His vocabulary, a medley of English and French, is half archaic and half slang.

In China, Monsignor Romier was an archbishop. After interminable molestations and brutal questioning and long imprisonment, he was expelled by the government of Mao Tse-tung. The archbishop was one of the 1,053 Church officials, missionaries, and nuns whom China had systematically deported in the course of the preceding year.

I met and talked with large numbers of those missionaries who had been forced to leave China after dedicating their whole lives to that country. Among these was the Italian missionary, Father Enaldi. He had cut out his own tongue with a razor blade to make sure that he would not betray the names of Chinese Catholics which the Communists were trying to extort from him by endless interrogation, applying the latest methods of psychological torture.

The stories those missionaries tell, taken together with

their written reports to the Congregation of the Propaganda at Rome, provide a detailed picture of the tactics used by the Mao government on the Chinese front of the great war between communism and the Catholic Church. In the Vatican's view, the Chinese front is among the major ones, though less on account of the number of Catholics involved than because of the "face" that is kept up for Christianity in Asia by the native congregations of the Church in China, many of which are very old.

Rome long ago created a local Chinese hierarchy. The first bishops in China, consecrated by Pope Pius XI, all were native Chinese, and China was the first of the nonwhite countries represented in the Sacred College. The large number of native bishops and priests form the hard core of the new religion in China. Catholicism has met with acceptance there—thus accounting for the violence of the Communist government's reaction. Following are the three stages of its anti-Catholic procedure:

First, it moves to break off the relationship between the Church in China and Rome. To that end, it puts on a campaign among the people, after which it expels the Pope's representative, Riberi, the Internuncio. The bishops are thus left isolated in China.

Secondly, it expels the bishops and the European and American missionaries, on the pretext that they are "engaging in espionage for the benefit of the capitalist reaction."

Thirdly, when a district has been deprived of its connections with Rome and of its non-Chinese religious leaders, strong pressure is put upon the native clergy to make the Catholic Church in China autonomous, national, and independent of the Vatican. In step with this, the seminaries are shut down or else placed under governmental supervision.

Wherever communism comes face to face with Catholicism, no matter in what land, its attack will be found to occur in these same three phases: separation from Rome, suppression of the episcopate, and assimilation through the intermediary of a national church.

In this connection, one is reminded of the violent campaign carried on by the Belgrade authorities against Monsignor Oddi, chargé of the nunciature in Yugoslavia, who left that country as a result of the severance of diplomatic relations. In Yugoslavia, as in Hungary and Rumania, the government gives semi-official encouragement to the formation of "independent" and "national" communions of Catholics. In countries behind the Iron Curtain, the nuncios have long since been forced to leave. The heads of the Catholic hierarchy are in jail or have been rendered powerless.

Sometimes the attack on the bishops takes an even more violent form. The prime example was the execution of Monsignor Bossilkov in Bulgaria. All Catholic bishops found in the territories under control of the U.S.S.R. have been either deported or jailed, as have the Uniat bishops of Galicia.

In Yugoslavia, the government has sponsored what are called "associations of people's priests." In writing of this, the State Secretariat said: "Police are present at those religious gatherings. Speeches are made in open and public condemnation of /the actions of bishops and even of the Church itself. These associations are linked in close collaboration with the People's Front and, through that as intermediary, with the Union of Yugoslav Communists."

Techniques for the creation of nationalist churches, always under close government supervision, may vary from country to country. In China, the nationalization proceeds through four phases, as follows:

1. Chinese Catholics are grouped, parish by parish, into schools or associations for men and for women. The units thus formed are called upon to take part in mass demonstrations. They have it explained to them, on the basis of texts from the Gospels or St. Paul, that they must be "obedient to them that are masters" or "render unto Caesar the things that are Caesar's."

2. Christians are obliged to attend "study clubs." These clubs are under the direction of "Christian progressives," who profess to be restoring to religion its "primitive purity." It is made clear how such-and-such a bishop or priest is prostituting his sacred calling to political ends. After which the members are indoctrinated with the rudiments of Marxist ideology.

3. When a certain number of Catholics have been brain-washed by the study clubs, the pace is stepped up. Huge protest meetings are organized against the foreign missionaries. The Legion of Mary, a Catholic Action society, is publicly charged with espionage, child murder, and so forth. The study clubs now spearhead a movement to reform the Church. The devout are urged to take sides against the priests and bishops in order to safeguard the purity of their faith.

4. It is at this point that the study clubs, which have formed communities of Christians, Mohammedans, and Buddhists, all under State "enlightenment," declare themselves ready to take over the administration of a parish or of the diocese, in place of the native pastors. "Purification" thus undergoes a transformation and comes

out "unification." The congregations of all the newly formed religious persuasions are incorporated into a species of super-religion on a nationalist base.

Thenceforth, whenever the government has to deal with matters of religion, it draws its expert operatives from among the "fully enlightened." Protestants, Mohammedans, Buddhists, and Catholics, progressives to a man and all controlled by their government, form leaderless religious groups, while bishops, priests, and their flocks, anxious to preserve the integrity of their faith, are treated as obstructionists inspired by hatred of the new regime.

Thus, in the very countries where her apostolic efforts have been the greatest, Rome sees the ranks of her priesthood depleted—and, what disturbs her even more, the reservoir of fresh recruits dried up at the source.*

---

* For the situation of the Church in China, see *L'Etoile contre la Croix*, by F. Dufay. (Hong Kong: Nazareth Press.)

The Swiss Guard in Belvedere Courtyard

The Pope on the Anniversary of His Coronation

XXVIII

The "Red Pope" Spreads the Word

THREE CENTURIES HAVE
passed since the central government of the Church took
in hand the work of Catholic expansion. The Pope entrusted the task to a Congregation especially founded to
pursue it, *De Propaganda Fide*. Prior to that centralization

of missionary effort, the Catholic apostolate was carried
forward by the great navigators as they set out to explore
the world. Missions were for a long while the monopoly
of Portugal and Spain; the work of missionaries being
made auxiliary to political expansion and turned to the
advantage of the mother countries, greedy for territory
and new wealth.

Following the foundation of the Propaganda, the
Popes established, in an old Roman palace on the Piazza
di Spagna, a sort of general headquarters for Catholic
forces setting out to overcome the heathen. From there,
at the present time, the Cardinal-Prefect of the Propaganda exercises command over an army of some twelve
thousand native and sixteen thousand missionary priests.
The number of Catholics under his jurisdiction totals
28,000,000, but of these the greater portion constitutes
only a bridgehead in the immense regions of Africa and
Asia, toward whose conversion Rome patiently proceeds.

Despite setbacks encountered by the Church in the
many areas exposed to Communist influence, the number
of the newly Christianized is steadily growing. In Africa,
the Propaganda had three million Catholics under its
jurisdiction in 1927. In 1949 there were eleven million.
In Asia, the number of Catholics grew from six million
to nine million. However, these figures are mere approxi-
mations, the changes having resulted not only from ac-
cessions to the ranks of the devout but also from administrative regrouping. Nevertheless the Church has high
hopes of expanding among the native populations that are
now gaining independence and making ready to take over
the helm from the older generation.

In the missionary field, the Church's trend is more and
more toward the establishing of national Churches, in

the sense of creating these around a cadre of native priests and bishops. This tendency runs clear back to the earliest days of missionary endeavor; but it was not until the pontificate of Pius XI that Rome, by a bold policy decision, took the calculated risk of including in the Church government Catholics recently converted by her missionaries. Today, in those areas, the Congregation of the Propaganda restricts itself to the barest staking-out of territory; after which it helps the young local Churches to find their own way step by step.

At the same time, the rival forces of that other religion, communism, are trying to strengthen their hold on the populations of Africa and Asia. And there we have the essential factor by which, in our own epoch, the Propaganda has been led to shift the basis of its technique. That factor is responsible also for the return of the Church's missions once again to the immediate direction of the Pope and the State Secretariat. Missionaries, now finding themselves face to face with the social problems of the emancipated peoples, are likewise confronted with nationalist or Marxist propaganda. Elsewhere, in many of the old countries of Europe, the seepage of de-Christianization makes it necessary to do missionary work in the very heart of the so-called civilized lands. A Mission to France or a Mission to Paris is organized, and the missionaries make their way into the factories of the great cities with the same zeal that animated those of old who set sail for parts unknown. Father Charles de Foucauld, who assumed the guise of the poorest of nomads in order, by compassionate and personal example, to carry the Christian message into the Arab world, has, since his death, become the inspiration and in effect the patron saint of a movement which bids fair to spread throughout

the old world. More especially, it may serve to carry forward the project begun by the worker-priests and their
successors.

This closer contact between Rome and the regional
African and Asian Christianities is a new venture in the
life of the Church. "Exotic" transformations into native
terms of the representation of Christ, the Virgin, and the
Saints already have been placed on view at exhibitions of
missionary work. In the field, attempts also are being made
—somewhat clumsily, it must be said—to create styles of
religious architecture adapted to local tastes; but it seems
likely that a deeper sort of union gradually will become
operative between the spiritual life of the new regional
populations and the Church of Rome. Until the present
time, conversion to Catholicism has been synonymous
with conversion to the Latin Rite and to Occidental modes
of thought and worship. But in its missionary enterprises
the Church is tending less and less toward the imposition
of whatever is distinctively Western.

Slowly, the Church is seeking out new means for the
expression of piety, and perhaps the day may come when
it will levy upon native contributions to enrich its own
rites. The question first was raised by Jesuit missionaries
to China, four centuries ago, when they proposed the
inclusion in Catholic liturgy of the reverence paid by
Chinese to the dead. After long controversy, it was decided at Rome that this suggestion was dangerous because
it would involve conceding legitimacy to a heathen cult.
But then, having reflected upon the matter, the Church,
after the passage of four hundred years, brought it up
again. By a decision which now dates back three decades,
the Sovereign Pontiff has authorized Chinese Catholics
to signalize their veneration of ancestors by outward ob-

servances. This veneration is held to be perfectly compatible with Catholic doctrine.

At the head of the Propaganda is placed a Cardinal-Prefect who sometimes is called, on account of his purple robe, the "Red Pope." The power he wields over the Catholic communities under his jurisdiction is very broad. When, as often happens, the congregations of those communities are constituted into dioceses and placed under government of bishops, representatives of the Cardinal-Prefect of the Propaganda then limit themselves to assisting and advising the budding hierarchies. In the stage preceding, the new Christian communities are run by Vicars Apostolic or Prefects Apostolic, or by Superiors of self-governing missions. In the East Indies, Japan, and China, and in vast expanses of Africa, native hierarchies of the conventional pattern already have been set up. From Alaska to the Antilles, from Liberia and Togoland to Yaunde and Nyassa and Zanzibar, from Port Louis to Madras and Colombo to Bangkok and Siwantze to Hiroshima, the Propaganda, its claims staked out and bridgeheads established, keeps close supervision over the work of its apostles and notes down, in the great and growing book of all its martyrs, the names of these, the latest witnesses to their Faith.

XXIX

Sackcloth à la Mode

VIA COLA DI RIENZO, NOT
far from St. Peter's, is one of the business streets of
Rome. Along it, through the morning rush of housewives,
a pair of nuns are threading their way. One is in her
sixties. Her features have the stern regularity of Gothic

sculpture. Her shorn head is imprisoned in a sort of starched helmet. A heavy black veil shrouds her shoulders and reaches clear down to her waist. Over her belt is looped a thick rosary and her voluminous black robe sweeps the sidewalk.

Her companion, who is hardly out of adolescence, is literally barefaced; a piece of light veiling, such as nurses wear, holds her back hair in place and comes down scarcely lower than the nape of her neck. She is wearing a short cape, a narrow white collar, and a black dress with hemline six inches from the ground. These are two sisters belonging to the Convent of Our Lady of Nazareth. One still wears the old-style habit. The other wears the new costume, as approved by the Pope from among those modeled before him by a parade of youthful nuns.

Ever since the Congregation of the Religious decided to modernize nuns' costumes, the sisterhoods have been in a great flutter. The quarrel between Ancients and Moderns has flamed up all over again. In the houses of the female religious, there is open warfare between the generations. The Moderns are finding themselves hard-pressed but they have the Pope on their side. Dress reform is whispering through the convents like a breath of fresh air. It is all very gradual, actually, since the Vatican intends not to force anything upon the religious communities, whose autonomy it is careful to respect.

"Have you heard that Schuberth—he's the dressmaker who costumes all the big music-hall stars—has run up a string of models for the nuns' new habits and submitted them to the Pope? Not much chance of his getting any action, though."

The man who made this remark to me is a leading tailor to the "sharpest" dressers of Rome—ecclesiastical Rome,

that is. We were chatting together in his showroom in
the shadow of the Pantheon and S. Luigi de' Francesi, a
neighborhood which is the Barclay Street of the Eternal
City for clerical-supply houses. Behind a panel of plate
glass, a magnificent red-beaver cardinal's hat. Silken capes
of violet, lavender, rose, and red, capes of ermine, of
corded silk, of silk brocade—all building up to an aura,
an atmosphere of unctuous and velvety richness. Unhappy
silks . . . poor little ermine! At the last Consistory, by the
Pope's decree, cardinals' trains are to be cut and the use
of fabrics *de luxe* is proscribed.

Dress reform, however, is merely a ripple on the surface,
an indication of deep undercurrents now stirring within
the vast and various ocean of the "Regulars," regardless
of cult or rule. This disturbance has to do with the situation of the religious of either sex in modern society.

"Just think," a Franciscan Father said to me, "that in
the midst of the Atomic Age we still go on living dressed
in burlap, like our Founder!"

We were at the Ciampino airport, outside Rome, and
the day was cold. I had on a heavy camel's-hair overcoat
and he was wearing sandals. They were made of strap-
work and he had on no stockings or socks. Down the
gaping neck of his habit poured the Roman *tramontana*.
But the glacial wind seemed not to bother the Franciscan.

"The first seven centuries are the hardest," he said with
a laugh.

Many of his confrères, though, throughout the orders,
are asking themselves nowadays whether it is fitting and
proper to wear medieval costume while going about their

work in the contemporary world of shorts and jet pro-
pulsion. In other words, how serviceable is it to appear
in such a world as living anachronisms, set apart from
one's contemporaries by even the clothes one wears?

In the sphere of their intellectual activities, a large
number of the religious communities have cut the question short and sent their shock troops out into the fore-
front of scientific and esthetic positions. But when it
comes to modifying the mere externals of the "regular"
existence, they have to wait upon the sanction of the
central government. The latter, as the Vatican tailor said
to me, is never in a hurry. And never less so than when,
as now, it becomes ruffled by a certain ebullience among
the younger generation of the regular clergy, eager to
"modernize" the Church, and braces itself to resist any
pressure for undue haste.

Monks and nuns belong to an infinity of orders and
live according to an infinite variety of rules. But there is
a sharp demarcation line between the "actives" and the
"contemplatives." While the former lead lives full of
activity—in schools, missions, hospitals, institutions of re-
education, the reclamation of prostitutes—the others are
buried away from the world. They lead a life devoted
almost wholly to prayer and self-denial. Their convents
are the Church's "reserve force"; and from time to time
they produce salient personalities whose influence is felt
for years or even centuries. Such was Thérèse of Lisieux,
a young girl hidden away in the Carmelite nunnery of a
little Normandy village, who became one of the outstanding personalities yet produced by the Church in the
twentieth century.

In the convents of the contemplatives, be they men or
women, life is rigorous in the extreme. Trappists, for
example, are not allowed to speak. A rudimentary sign

language, picked up during the novitiate, is the Fathers'
only means of intercommunication. Fasting takes the
severest possible forms. The offices of religion follow one
another for hours on end. Slumber is broken in the middle
of the night for services of prayer in a chapel which
more often than not is freezing cold. And all the while
the strictest intellectual and spiritual discipline is demanded, entailing absolute obedience to the Superiors
and a communal existence with individuals not of one's
own choosing whom it is often next to impossible for
one to like.

"Our order," so Dom François-Régis Jammes, abbot of
the Trappist monastery of Sept-Fons, told Roland Cluny,
"wishes only to let the world see the forgotten face of
the Early Church, the fraternal society where everything
was held in common. It sounds like the simplest of under-
takings—yet how hard it really is! You must realize that
we never know the meaning of solitude except during our
private prayers, which leave us alone with God. We work,
eat, sleep, and serve the Lord together, always. It sounds
like nothing. Try it! Bring together a group of a hundred
men and compel them to live constantly in one another's
company, in the same house, engaged in the same tasks,
coming together at the same hour into the same refectory,
the same dormitory, with their assorted characters which,
be they never so good, have their rough edges, their con-
trarieties, their obsessions—yes, and their bodies, which
often are laden with infirmities. Never will you bring
them to the point of merely abiding one another, let alone
of loving—forever considerate and at every instant ready
to yield to and encourage and assist one another without
one frown of ill humor, ever, or gesture of impatience, or
selfish withdrawal, or even so much as a mute reproach.
Yet that is what Christ expects and demands of us, each

and every one, when he reminds us that God's commandment is to love our neighbor as ourself."

While Trappists are condemned to live perpetually in common, Carthusians choose permanent solitude. Each dwells in a tiny cottage and leaves it only to attend communal offices in the convent church. Twice daily his meals are delivered through a wicket. Apart from the passing-by of the lay brother on his rounds and silent encounters with the other monks during religious offices, the Carthusian has no human contacts. His whole life is devoted to prayer and contemplation. "He rises," to quote once more from Roland Cluny, "at eleven o'clock at night. His bedtime is at seven. He kneels before the cross, repeats matins and lauds from the Office of the Holy Virgin, and, leaving his cottage shortly before midnight, without a sound he treads in his white list slippers along the cloister where glide other shadows. He remains in the church, in his stall, until half-past two, singing the offices appointed for the night. He returns to his cell and there he says prime according to the Shorter Office; and he lies down again upon his cot at the stroke of three. Not quite four hours later, arising once more, he resumes his solitary vigil to intone prime under his breath from the Full Canon and tierce from the Holy Virgin.

"It is getting on for eight o'clock when his morning orisons are completed. Along the cloister, now dappled with sunshine, he hurries a second time to the church and attends the conventual Mass prior to saying his own in private. It is ten o'clock before he returns to his cottage, where at last he has a few moments of respite before the exercises and sacred readings that take up the interval between sext and nones from the Holy Virgin. Half an hour before noon he is at his stack to chop wood, and from there he goes to his carpentry bench or to weed his garden. He goes up to his bedroom at noon, says nones as appointed for the day, and then goes down and takes from the hatch his one daily meal, which is always scant.

"At two o'clock, having done his housework, he opens a book and studies it to find food for meditation. Three o'clock: back to his workshop. Three-thirty: he says vespers from the Shorter Office. Three forty-five: he goes to the church for the last time that day, sings communal vespers, and returns half an hour later to his cell, which he will not leave again until evening. Another hour of study. At 5:15 he finds at his hatch the hunk of bread and measure of watered wine that will serve him in lieu of supper. Lastly, at six o'clock, he makes his examination of conscience, followed by extremely long orisons and by compline, which the others are softly intoning along with him in the depths of their retreats. It is seven o'clock. His day is ended. He lies down and goes to sleep. And this goes on his whole life long—which, among Carthusians, is often very long indeed—until the moment of last repose in the cemetery full of black crosses, not one of which bears a name.*

Cloistered nuns, in every country of the world, are living under varied rules which often are more stringent than those for men. Occasionally, the great monastic orders that combine contemplation and action both, such as the Benedictines and the Dominicans, form affiliated

---

* Roland Cluny, *Sous le froc et la bure*. (Editions du Témoignage Chrétien: Paris, 1953.)

sisterhoods which vow themselves exclusively to prayer and meditation. Various writings, from time to time, reporting mystical visions and profound spiritual experiences, issue anonymously from such convents; and one may form from them some impression of the depth of the inner life that goes on there, silently and in secret. And occasionally, too, among the cloistered nuns, the Church discovers a new saint and proceeds with her canonization, albeit not until some while after she has been buried in her convent cemetery.

Lined up in opposition to this silent army of contemplatives stand the troops of the "regulars" who wish not only for action but to be active out in the world. The Jesuits already have done away with convents, the communal saying of offices, and a habit distinctive from the attire of priests. Our day is witnessing the emergence of tendencies that are more radical still. The life conventual is beginning to seem too far removed from reality, too harsh, too formalized. Catholics who have the "vocation" feel forced outward instead. Communities are forming wherein the monastic life is, so to speak, clandestine: where the members of the community dress like you and me, take the same subway, and lean the elbow on the same mahogany. According to Scriptural commandment, one should be *in* this world but not *of* it. In their hidden chapel, these clandestine monks or, as the case may be, secretive sisters, carry out the religious exercises prescribed by their respective rules with all the collective concentration of their elders.

XXX

The Pope Mobilizes the "Regulars"

AT THE SAME TIME WHEN
problems of modernizing the apostolate were being de-
bated, there took place at Rome a most unusual event in
Church history: a world congress of all the monastic
orders, who were requested by the Pope to "adapt their

mode of existence to the demands of contemporary life."

Nothing could have been more picturesque than the vast hall of the Palace of the Chancellery where members of the congress conducted their deliberations in secret meetings from which the unsanctified were rigorously shut out. Dressed in habits of the most variegated cut and color, they had converged upon Rome from monasteries at the world's end or from the strictest seclusion. Present there (and at the subsequent congress, held by the female religious) were representatives of 1,200,000 men and women trained by round-the-clock discipline and tempered by the sternest of asceticism as practiced in obedience to the triple vow, or three commandments, of Chastity, Poverty, and Obedience.

The brotherhoods gave themselves over, in Latin and the principal modern tongues, to a protracted session of unsparing self-criticism. Some went so far as to say: "Our habits are an absurdity in the modern world, and so are our tonsures. We are too widely scattered, too disunited. Our superiors ought to show more respect for our personalities. Our stewards do not know how to administer a household or render a proper accounting. We give too much thought to maintaining the prestige of our order. We do not see clearly enough the 'big picture' of the Catholic Front. We lack initiative and live too much according to routine."

Above and beyond this self-critical exchange of views, however, was the Pope's own request to the heads of the Great Orders, pressing them to start an urgent "updating." What drove the Pope to this proposal for reorganization was, yet again, that ever-present feeling, which seems uppermost in his mind, of the imminent threat presented to the Church by the activity of its enemies and by the anti-church, the counter-religion of communism, above all. In addressing the brotherhoods, the Pope stressed, as he so often does, that we are living nowadays in a state of emergency.

"After the long vicissitudes of the late war," wrote Pius XII in his Encyclical *Menti nostri* (September 23, 1950), "the number of priests, whether in Catholic lands or in the mission field, no longer is sufficient to meet the constantly growing need." It was for this reason that the Pope, when calling the congress, had informed the Regulars that he intended to summon them to take their stand among the active forces of the Catholic clergy. When it came, his summons was directed to the contemplatives as well: "All, even those of the religious who live withdrawn and in silence, must contribute to the effectiveness of the priestly apostolate by prayer and sacrifice, and those who can, by action."

Paraphrasing the Pope's words, Cardinal Piazza, one of his close associates in this attempted modernization of the conventual life, exhorted the assembled religious in these terms:

"Come out of doors! That would seem to be the Sovereign Pontiff's mandate to all who are not explicitly prevented by laws of seclusion or bound by other such firm pledges as are incompatible with apostolic endeavor. When the house is burning, everybody must run to put out the fire—and is not that the urgency of the present moment?" And the Cardinal continued: "When you look at existing religious orders in the light of today, do you find all of them adapted to the demands of modern

missionary and social work? Right there we have the
basic question that confronts this congress. To find the
answer, you must proceed to an examination of conscience, a revision of structure and methods, and possibly
to several bold reforms."

Many members of the congress brought forward pro-
posals at Rome for the adaptation of monastic life to
present-day needs. Notable was Dom Pierre Basset, abbot
of St. Martin de Ligugé, who declared: "The exhaustion
of the capitalistic system makes it obligatory for religious
orders to revise their economic basis. The drying-up of
official patronage and the declassification of social groups
render the isolation of religious houses more precarious.
The outward observances traditional to the religious life
no longer bear witness to the truth so impressively as
they once did—not when, as now, they are confronted
by a society divided between the pursuit of comfort and
the endurance of undeserved misery."

For his part, Father Robert Svoboda contributed an
analysis of what he called the "growing anticlericalism
inside the Church, together with the resistance one finds
to any reform within the orders."

Father Bernard Kelly had this to say. "Modern man
tends to reject the advances of the religious precisely in
proportion to the degree in which we fail to approach
him in a manner which he can judge in purely human
terms. It is clear that some adaptation to such terms is
desirable and necessary since we religious have no right
to doom our labors to unfruitfulness. Typical of such
adaptation would be to wear—or not to wear—a distinctive religious habit, and to take a more or less active part
in economic and cultural and social organizations."

The congress also heard from Father Wilhelm Schamoni

a report of experiences he had had while at Dachau. He had been subjected to a long interrogation about other priests who were in the concentration camp and what deviations and errors of vocation they had revealed to him. Father Schamoni had been in contact at Dachau with thousands of the religious brought in from many different dioceses and orders. He had formed, he said, a general impression that many priests "have not grasped, in seminary or convent, the fact that the central problem of the religious life is utter self-abnegation."

The Congress of Rome that bore down so severely upon the inward shortcomings of seminaries and convents was followed, at the express invitation of the Congregation of the Religious, by a series of other regional and national meetings. Such assemblies were held, in recent years, in the United States, Italy, Bolivia, Colombia, Brazil, the Argentine, France, Canada, and South Africa.

In this whole process, heaviest emphasis is placed upon the readaptation of the female communities.

A surprising number of convents of the contemplative religious live in a state of want bordering on famine. Many of those houses are seldom sure of their daily bread. Heating is to them an unknown luxury and their buildings stand open to the elements. The general drift of economic conditions, the drying-up of bequests, and the war, which ravaged buildings and real estate and ruined benefactors, are sufficient to account for the material decay of many such convents. Often, they have subsisted upon daily wages of their lay sisters, who are not tied down by long religious offices and meditations; but manual labor of that sort no longer pays, and besides, in many of the communities, chronic undernourishment renders the sisters incapable of the sustained exertion required of them by today's living. However, in many countries, the number of convents of cloistered nuns is on the increase.

At Rome, the Congregation of the Religious does nothing to encourage the foundation of fresh communities. On the contrary. By order of the Pope, there now are being created "federations" within which will be incorporated some houses of the religious whose rules of life are similar. That will permit a general housecleaning of their economy and the "up-dating" (to use an expression very popular with the Congregation) of their rule itself.

The Congress of the Sisterhoods conducted a detailed discussion, under guidance of the Congregation, of the problems presented by convents of women in our time. In numerous reports confessors and nuns minutely examined the psychology of the Catholic young girl who has "vocation." Speakers harped upon imperfections in the training of novices and the ignorance that often obtains inside the convents. The congress even went so far as to propose the establishment at Rome of a School for Superiors to which the future directresses of nunneries could be sent by the principal orders.

The Pope in person lavished advice upon the sisterhoods in congress assembled, and ventured even to discuss details of dress. "As for the garment of religion, choose one that shall be the expression of your inward simplicity and of religious modesty; it then will be an object of edification to all, including modern youth. . . .

"The sense of the constitutions generally, when interpreted according to the letter and the spirit, smooths the way of the female religious to the accomplishment of the tasks that are to make of her a good preceptress and educator for our times. One may see that in the purely technological domain. For instance, in many lands, the sisters avail themselves of it in the manner most convenient—such as the bicycle, if the work requires. At the outset, that was a startling departure, but it was not contrary to the rule. It is possible that certain details of the usage of the times, certain prescriptive matters which are no more than applications of the rule, certain practices which were in accordance with bygone circumstances but which serve only to hamper the educational work, ought to be adapted to our times."

Not a single problem relevant to the young girl on her way to becoming a young religious was declared taboo in the general debates: the value of virginity and of the religious vocation, and the psychic and moral balance of the youthful religious "who often does not, until later on, become fully aware of the precise content of her vows of perfect chastity"; struggle against scruples; personal friendships; necessity of allowing the religious full freedom to keep up with the evolution of the modern world (and in this connection, the Reverend Father Liévain's report protests against expurgation, censorship, the prohibition of certain movies, etcetera); modification of discipline ("Are certain traditional forms of asceticism any longer timely? For instance, humiliations?"); diet, number of hours' sleep, medical examination, warmth, and hygiene ("Let the religious be allowed full liberty to provide for their personal cleanliness as diligently as they did in the world").

Little by little, these reforms unquestionably will spread despite the misgivings they arouse among cloistered old-timers of both sexes. And yet we must ask ourselves just how far the Congregation of the Religious will succeed in implementing the Pope's suggestions in favor of "adaptation" to modern life when it comes to the contemplative orders. For it does appear that, in accordance with the "dynamism" actually animating it, the present generation is conscious of a strong need for revival of the spiritual life. There never was a time when mystical (or pseudomystical) experiences have been so much sought after. Side by side with the expressed eagerness of numerous clerics to come out into the world and do battle, one hears within the Church a call for the contemplative life in its severest forms. We are witnessing a transvaluation of values within the Church. The more intimate participation of the laity in its inner life is arriving hand-in-hand with a renewal of Catholic mysticism.

XXXI

Catholic Action Today

A CATHOLIC KIKUJU FROM
the Mau-Mau country was one of the most prominent
leaders in the Congress for Catholic Action organized in
Central Africa by Signor Vittorino Veronese.

At St. Calixtus, the huge palace close beside S. Maria

in Trastevere, where it enjoys the extra-territorial status reserved to buildings owned by the Vatican, this friendly lawyer from Verona occupies two or three rooms where he houses his files and his small secretarial staff. Signor Veronese's offices bear the name, Permanent Committee for Congresses. Their work is under direct control of the State Secretariat, in Monsignor Dell'Acqua's section. What it represents is the embryonic beginning of an international organization for Catholic Action.

Signor Veronese, who is a man of moderation and common sense, restricts himself at the present time to the widest possible practice of personal diplomacy. Frontiers no longer exist for him. He lives in plane and train. From UNESCO to the spectacular meetings of an International Eucharistic Congress, from Pax Romana (an international organization of university students) to the F.O.A., there is not one major international corporate group, Catholic or non-Catholic, at which he fails to put in an appearance. Before starting to organize at and from the center it is important, in his opinion, to count your effectives and fit them into the international scheme. Nor is it any part of the Committee's or the State Secretariat's plan to centralize and unify to death the Catholic Action movements, which are of the widest variety and have to work under circumstances as different as can be conceived.

It was Signor Veronese's service branch that instituted, during the last Holy Year, for the first time in the history of the Church, a World Congress for the Lay Apostolate.

Called together at Rome, that congress passed in review the thousands of Catholic Action organizations of every sort. At the same time, it drew up a basic list of international organizations. These run the gamut from the International Council of the Marian Apostolate to the

International Catholic Association of Girls' Protective Leagues, from the World Union of Catholic Philosophical Societies to the Bureau of the National Catholic Welfare Conference (U.S.A.) for United Nations Affairs. Up until the World Congress for the Lay Apostolate, this multiplicity of international Catholic associations had been loosely interconnected through the Conference of Presidents, which after 1952 became the Conference of International Catholic Organizations.

To this organism, which is a sort of ectoplasm of the various associations, the Vatican has linked the Permanent Committee for Congresses. The latter's duties are to lay the ground periodically for great international or regional congresses of laymen, to assemble the documentation covering the activities of Catholic organizations, and to set up a study bureau to collate that documentation. In short, Signor Veronese's main task lies in the establishing of contacts between the organizations working on the fringes of the State Secretariat.

International Catholic Action got its start after the last war as a consequence of the development of international organisms with which the Church plans active collaboration. Among the resolutions adopted by the World Congress for Laymen, where seventy-four countries and thirty-eight Catholic international organizations were represented, one notes in particular: "Catholics shall take part in the life of existing organizations and institutions in order to assure the presence in them of the leaven of Christianity."

Although in theory every one of the Catholic organizations ought to be administratively and financially self-sufficient, a reorganization so sweeping as that projected by Signor Veronese can not be carried through without sizable funds. Those the Vatican was in no position to provide. The difficulty has been got around by creating the Pius XII Foundation, with the Holy See placing a sum at the Foundation's disposal to prime the pump; but the greater part will have to be raised through subsidies which will be solicited from Catholics all over the world. The endowment thus created will be managed by a five-man administrative council appointed by the State Secretariat.

We have seen the manner in which the Popes have gone about the tightening of their grasp upon the levers of control over the Catholic hierarchy. But now another problem of like kind confronts them: the direction of the laity.

The entire system of the hierarchy with all its ramifications is not adequate to fulfill the tasks that lie in the way of today's Church, and the Popes of recent years have loudly proclaimed that action by the laity must be brought in to help.

To implement this, the Church is proceeding with great caution. For what is implied is the inclusion of lay action within the Church in the most intimate manner possible. Protestantism attempted to do just that, long since, with the result that the whole hierarchical structure was demolished and the various Churches were brought under sway of the secular power. In our own day, the experiment of the worker-priests (inspired in part, no doubt, by the action of militant Catholics in the factories) was tending, in some cases, toward a secularization of the priestly office. From the outset, therefore, the Popes have been mindful never to relax the grip of the hierarchy upon the organizing of Catholic Action. It has been put directly under the orders of the bishops in the dioceses and of the Pope in the Church as a whole. An ecclesiastical assistant to the lay directors is obligatory. Catholic Action is, as Pius XII told the World Congress of Laymen, "a tool in the hands of the hierarchy, and should be like an extension of its arm."

The limits of Catholic Action differ according to the countries where it obtains. Missionary work is its purpose and Pius XII recurs again and again to the perils of the age and the necessity of mobilizing all the forces of Catholicism. Wherefore laymen are requested not only to take over—particularly in lands beyond the Iron Curtain —the instruction of children in the absence of priests, and to make known in their vicinity the "proper way of Catholic thinking," but also to lead the fight in every domain of political and social life.

"Necessarily and continually," so Pius XII told the Congress of Laymen, "the life of man finds itself in touch with the law and spirit of Christ; there results from this, by the force of things, a reciprocal interpenetration of the religious apostolate and political action. Politics, in the basic sense of the word, means nothing more than collaboration for the welfare of the City (*Polis*). But this welfare of the City extends far and wide, and consequently it is in the field of politics that are disputed and likewise decreed the laws that are of highest importance, such as those concerning marriage, the family, the child, the school, to limit ourselves to examples in point. Are not those the very questions that engage before all else the interest of religion? We have, in an earlier allocution (that of May 3, 1951), traced the delimitation between Catholic Action and political action. Catholic Action

ought not to enter the lists of political party strife. But, as
We also said to the members of the Olivetan Conference,
'laudable though it is to hold one's self above the adventi-
tious quarrels that embittered the strife of parties, . . .
equally reprehensible is it to leave the field free for the
unworthy or incapable to take over direction of the
affairs of State' (March 28, 1948). Up to what point can
and should the apostle stay within this limitation? On
that, it is hard to formulate a uniform rule for everyone.
Circumstances and mentalities are not everywhere the
same."*

---

* Italian Catholic Action, which Pius XII follows with close attention,
is guided by its president, Sig. Luigi Gedda, toward direct intervention
in politics, and especially toward the struggle against communism. Under
his initiative, the leaders have tried to establish a network of "missionary
bases" patterned after the cell system of the Communists. Signor Gedda's
aggressiveness has led to several outbursts of criticism and to rebellion
in a sector of the ranks.

XXXII

Toward a Lay Apostolate

THE GREAT IMPETUS TO Catholic Action occurred under the pontificate of Pius XI. It appears that the reign of Pius XII will be notable for a related event of importance to Catholicism: the accession of the laity to a more active life within the Church.

Through Catholic Action, the hierarchy (Pope, bishops, and the priests) created a tool which prolonged their arm. The devout of the congregations were confined to their rôle as auxiliaries. They were under control of the clergy. That subordination, however, gave rise to not a little restiveness, which became more noticeable after the harsh experiences of the war years when priests and laymen had found themselves shoulder to shoulder, threatened by the same dangers and exercising like responsibilities.

It was then that Catholics, practicing their faith in a world cut clean across by hatred, began by degrees to grow conscious of the part that was once more becoming rightfully theirs in the general conduct of the Church. The reason for this was not alone the fact that many such laymen were called upon to write their profession of faith in their own blood throughout the many lands where the Church was persecuted (and still is). There was also the fact that their slightest gestures took on the character of testimony to that faith; and that the involvement required of them went beyond the mere plane of any social or political action and included the whole man. Gradually, they ceased to be a purely passive element and shared actively in the building-up of the Church, at that time when everything seemed in need of being started again *de novo*, as in Early Christian days. Laymen came then to perceive that they formed as of full right a part of that mystical body of the Church about which theologians had lectured them so much; that, as things stood, the Church was composed of two distinct elements, priests and parishioners, and that the Christian community was incomplete unless the laity participated in it as much as did the clergy.

Timed exactly right to draw attention, there appeared in France a thick tome which immediately caused a profound stir beneath the surface of Catholic life: *Landmarks for a Theology of the Laity,* by the Dominican Father Yves Congar.* I shall here briefly present a few of the points it makes.

The Catholic world is little by little coming to recall that an "order" of laymen exists and that it may rightfully be set side by side with the priestly order. Vocation, in the sense of a summons from God, no longer necessarily means a vocation to the priesthood or the cloister. One may respond to it while remaining in the world. Whereas clerics and the religious are of the Church only, laymen feel themselves to be "of the world and of the Church." Their "secular involvement" completes the hierarchic apostolate. They perceive that without them the Church would not be at all, or would be incomplete.

Numerous signs of this new spirit—or rather, of this return to ancient experience—have long foretold such an evolution of the laity; the liturgical movement, for example. There long has been a reaction going on in the Church against the estrangement of the devout from participation in religious offices.

The priest, in the Latin Rite, by an evolution centuries in the making, turns his back to the congregation, says prayers under his breath in a language the people do not understand, and performs the gestures essential to the sacrifice in a manner hardly visible or understandable. A great impulse of sentiment is gradually bringing about the elimination of these distortions. Altars are being turned again to face the people (or they are, at any rate, in numerous churches that are in the van), congregations

---
* Editions du Cerf, 1953.

say together and aloud the responses to the words of the celebrant, and the very "style" of the celebration of the office is changing. The gestures are becoming broad and slow, the speech distinct. Radio and especially television are revealing the details of the ritual to everyone and the participation of the devout is taking on ever more awareness. They are the ones who understand the symbolic meaning of the Church's rule by which priests are forbidden to celebrate the Mass if no one assists at it. The Mass, in short, is made for the congregation.

Another stage of this fresh awakening of awareness is signalized by a more profound and widespread comprehension of marriage. It is perceived to be like the first "Church cellule." For all Catholics, marriage is a Sacrament, and it is the espoused themselves who administer it, the priest being only a witness assigned by the Church. Thus, in the marriage rite, the espoused participate in one of the sacramental activities of the Church. At the moment when they plight their troth, they create a new community in Christ, and Catholic theology holds their union to be symbolic of that between the whole Church and Christ, its Head. And so likewise does this Sacrament, which in its essence is of the laity, exemplify the high dignity of the part reserved in the Church to the congregation.

"The Church issues a pressing summons to laymen, just as she does to the regular clergy. The urgency of the tasks to be performed and the perils of the age compel her to this mobilization. In a great many of his allocutions, the Pope proclaims that the number of priests is

insufficient and that it is necessary to relieve this need by
sending into action, each in his own order and according
to his powers, the regular clergy and the laymen. Gather
in, then, the unbelievers through the presence and the
action, in those places that are cut off from the Church,
of a Christian laity, jointly and severally of this world,
in the midst of which, bearing witness to Christ and to
His Charity, they shall fulfill in ever-growing measure the
mission of evangelization that He confides to His Church."
So writes the Plenary Assembly of the French Episcopate in its doctrinal declaration of 1954.

It is by such means, then, that the Church, recovering
its communal character, is making a vital experiment upon
that mystic body which, for the devout, it represents.
This evolution, of which many a priest is as fully aware
as are the laymen, does not always go forward without
peril to the Church. The experiment of the worker-priests,
as I remarked above, might readily have deviated toward
the secularization of the priestly office.

Precisely as they had laid aside their cassocks, the better
to identify themselves with their environment, so sometimes they came to feel that the celebration of the Mass
or the reading of the breviary carried implicit factors
making for "otherness." A laborer does not say Mass.

What came then into question was not a material im-
possibility but a principle which Rome could do nothing
but condemn. The priestly character, the special imprint
that a priest bears, are in effect inviolable and the work
proper to the priesthood ought to take precedence over
all other. A priest can not with impunity lay aside what
is the mainspring of his actions. And that essential element is the Eucharistic Sacrifice. It has seemed to the
investigators from Rome that in thus giving way on

certain essential points of their outward life, the worker-priests were running the risk of allowing themselves to be led on to the abandoning of the substantive elements of that very doctrine which they desired to preach. Their wish to identify themselves with their fellows drove them to give over their purely apostolic attitude in order to join the workers on the platform of social, labor-union, and political action. In laying aside the primacy of their priestly calling and in neglecting the urgency of their sacramental work, it was, according to the Roman investigators, toward a sort of protestantism that certain of the worker-priests were in danger of allowing themselves to gradually drift.

But such perils arise only in a few exceptional instances. The Catholic hierarchy jealously guards its prerogatives as handed down by the Apostolic tradition and the members of the congregations keep watch with an equally ardent insistence over theirs. The pressure of the laymen toward an equal sharing in the work of the Church will not "laicise" it but will, on the contrary, serve to waft it on its way.

This communal or ecumenical conception is very close to that which has steadily survived among the congregations of the dissident Eastern Churches. It also contitutes what is most in conformity with the Christian tradition in the numerous sects of Protestantism. The evolution of the Catholic laity may create a climate favorable to efforts toward reconciliation among the Christian Churches.

Part Seven

THE PAPAL SUCCESSION

XXXIII

The Pope Is Dead

WE RETURN TO THE SIS-
tine Chapel once again. That somber setting, where
Michelangelo's enormous fresco glows, is the recurrent
scene of the Church's hours of high drama. When the
Pope dies, the Conclave assembles there. And then it is

that the cardinals, fulfilling the most solemn of their duties, justify before the world their title as Princes of the Blood. For, as they there elect the Head of the Church and Vicar of Christ, each one of them is potentially the Pope.

The Pope, amid ritual pomp, is breathing his last. And, for one last time in that existence composed of contradictions, the extremes of humiliation and of grandeur coincide. Ill and worn out, as is almost invariably the case, by superhuman exertions and relentless tension round the clock, the Pontiff, no longer able to leave his room, took to his bed. All signs of the official residence have disappeared from his private apartment. Filled with the depressing apparatus of the sickroom, his bedchamber is the cell of a dying monk.

Kneeling about the door, the little group of the Pope's intimates now hear a powerful voice intoning Latin phrases. It is the Sacrista, a high prelate whose task it is to repeat the prayers for the dying:

"O most merciful Jesus, lover of souls, by the agony of Thy Most Sacred Heart and by the sorrows of Thine Immaculate Mother, wash with Thy blood the sinners of the whole world who are in agony and who shall this day pass into the life hereafter. O agonizing Heart of Jesus, have pity upon the dying."

It is also the prelate's office to administer Extreme Unction to the Pope. Besides the members of his family, who now are sent for, the ceremony is attended by the Pope's household staff, his doctors, assistants, and often by some of the cardinals and the generals of the religious orders.

When the Pope has yielded up the ghost, the doctor

approaches and certifies that he is dead. Then, falling
upon their knees, the prelates who are in the room say
together the prayers for the newly departed. Whereafter,
in due order of precedence, they all draw near and kiss
the Sovereign Pontiff's right hand.

Meanwhile, the news has already leaked out, and the
huge Palace of the Vatican is thrown into a sudden turmoil. Both panels of the chamber door are opened wide.
The *cameriere secreto* on duty—he is one of the household
prelates—covers the face of the deceased with a white
sheet. And already the canons-penitentiary, the confessors
attached to the basilica, are at hand. Theirs is the age-old
privilege of standing the first watch over the Pope's body.

Already, too, in the private chapel or perhaps before a
portable altar set up in the room itself, a ranking prelate
has begun the Mass for the repose of the soul of the Head
of the Church. Hour after hour the Masses succeed one
another, repeated in low tones by the chief dignitaries of
the Church and by the Pontiff's close friends.

Within the room, after all the doors have been closed,
proceeds the first ritual dressing of the body. The Pope
is attired in a white-silk cassock with a long train. A cape
of crimson velvet trimmed with ermine covers his shoulders. Upon his head is placed a velvet cap of the same
hue. A great pall of red silk is draped over the whole bed,
covering the body up to the chin. But the arms are left
outside and the ring, symbolic of the Papal power, is in
plain sight.

At the foot of the bed stand four lighted candles. With
clanking scabbards, two members of the Noble Guards
stride into the room and station themselves on either side
of the bed, their swords drawn. Between these two gold-

helmeted giants, the withdrawn profile of the old man lying there looks more humble and affecting than ever.

The Chamberlain or, if that post is vacant, the Dean of the Sacred College, now enters the room. To signalize the added dignity with which he is endowed—since he will, for a few days, be the highest authority in the Church—he is attended by a detachment of Swiss Guards bearing halberds. He has come to make official recognizance of the Pope's body. In this ceremony he is joined by the Vice-Chamberlain and the ranking members of the Apostolic Chamber. These last, who at one time held great power, have nowadays lost practically all their importance. They regain it, however, when a Pontiff dies. For it is they who act *ad interim* as trustees of the property and temporal rights of the Holy See.

The Chamberlain (or the Dean), kneeling before the mortal remains of the Pope, intones the *De Profundis.* Whereupon, approaching the bedside, he lifts the veil that shrouds the features and formally identifies the deceased. The practice of rapping three times with an ivory gavel upon the forehead of the defunct and calling him thrice by name has of late years been discontinued.

Only after official recognizance of the death does the Maître de Chambre draw the Fisherman's ring from the Pope's hand. Until this gesture is performed, the Pope, even in death, has continued to be regarded as invested with his power. Several days later this ring will be smashed in the course of one of the "general congregations" of the cardinals. A notary of the Apostolic Chamber draws up an affidavit certifying all these acts, which are vital to the legitimacy of the succession.

Now the palace, the basilica, and the hordes of the

devout lay claim to the Pontiff's body. A solemn procession of the corpse is expected to be held on the very day of death. As twilight falls, the cortege silently assembles.

A sergeant of the Swiss Guards in sparkling steel breastplate heads the procession. He is followed by footmen in red damask, officers of the Guard, Papal secretaries, chief dignitaries of the Papal Court, and generals of the Noble Guards in dress uniform. And then the Pope. His body reposes upon a litter borne by eight of the Noble Guards. Prelates bearing tall yellow candles form a guard of honor on either side. Immediately following are the cardinals, wearing violet copes. They are followed by the whole diplomatic corps. And at the end of the procession are monks representing the great religious orders. With their gaunt frames and somber habits of coarse wool, they seem to have stepped straight out of the surrounding frescoes, which the twilight has now dimmed.

Silently the procession files into the candle-lit Sistine Chapel. The figure of Christ in the "Last Judgment" stands out as a patch of brightness amid the blessed and the damned. Before the high altar is a catafalque draped with red silk. The remains are placed upon it, high above the heads of the living.

The first wave of the devout comes flooding into the chapel. The murmuring of prayers and psalms drones on into the late evening.

As night draws in, the doors are closed to the devout and there begins a fresh arraying of the body. It is done by the Penitentiaries of St. Peter's. The remains are being

made ready for the Sovereign Pontiff's last solemn entry
into his cathedral, where the populace will pay him their
final homage. This time the Pope will wear the full ceremonial vestments of his office, and it is thus that he will
be laid to rest.

A long white alb reaching to the feet goes over the
cassock. Over the alb, the penitentiaries adjust a red-and-
gold dalmatic and a great red chasuble. A full cape of
white silk shot with gold—the pluvial—covers the Pope's
shoulders. About his neck and down the length of his
body are unrolled the bands of white wool forming the
pallium, which only the Pope, the patriarchs, and primates
are entitled to wear. (The pallium is woven by a sisterhood of nuns, who jealously guard the privilege, from
the fleece of lambs blessed in the ancient Church of St.
Agnes, at Rome. The bands are placed to lie overnight
upon the tomb of St. Peter. They then are sent to the
Pope, who, upon the urgent demand of his prelates, hands
them out to those upon whom he chooses to confer the
"plenitude" of the exercise of episcopal powers.) The
Pope now also wears the special maniple reserved for the
Pontiff alone when he celebrates Mass. Of white silk
interwoven with threads of red and gold, it symbolizes
the union of the Western and Eastern Churches.

A tall golden miter crowns his head. Red gloves are
slipped upon his hands, and upon the right a ring of bril-
liants. His feet are shod with red slippers ornamented
with gold crosses and embroidered with gold thread.

Thus attired in ceremonial vestments, which symbolize
not only the dignities of the Papal office but all the
sacerdotal powers of the Church, the Pope is ready for
his final apotheosis. And here, amid flaring torches, he

will remain through the night, watched over by the frescoes of the "Last Judgment." The penitentiaries stand watch about him, and likewise the Noble Guards, who never leave the body for an instant; for it has been entrusted to their especial care from the moment the Head of the Church breathed his last.

On the morrow, a second great cortege forms in front of the Sistine Chapel. The full hierarchy of the Church now stands in line: the Sacred College, bishops, generals of the orders, canons; all high officials of the Household, which is to say, the Papal Court; detachments of all arms of the pontifical soldiery, and the representatives of all countries maintaining diplomatic relations with the Holy See. Dressed in red, the *sediari* head the procession, carrying torches to light the way through the vast hall where the cortege must pass to reach the royal stairway leading down to the basilica.

The cortege moves off amid a silence broken only by a murmuring here and there of the *De Profundis*. Detachments of guards palatine and the Swiss loom out of the shadows, their weapons clashing as they salute the body passing by. Gigantic Swiss halberdiers, armor-clad and helmeted, march on either side of it. Candles borne by the canons-penitentiary cast shimmers of yellow light upon the naked steel of blades and breastplates.

As the bearers of the Sovereign Pontiff start down the broad and echoing marble stairway, they tilt the litter in such a way that the body seems almost vertical against the red draperies of the bed. The tall golden miter gleams among the shadows and the red chasuble is a darker patch amid the violet robes and burnished armor.

And so the Pope is borne into the basilica. For the first

time no blast of silver trumpets, no plaudits of the crowd hail his entry. The immense church is empty and hung with black.

Before continuing on his way toward the tomb of the Prince of the Apostles, the Pope, as always, pauses within the Chapel of the Holy Sacrament. His mortal remains will repose there for three days. The Pope's face is turned toward the high screen that will hold in check the devout who come flooding past the entrance to the chapel. The Pope is laid upon a sort of inclined plane so that his head and the upper part of his body can be viewed from a distance. The feet reach almost to the grillwork; but nowadays the crowd no longer can kiss them, as formerly, according to the Italian custom.

Next morning, as soon as it is day, the entire city comes trooping to view its bishop. The blasé Romans, who always find the pomp and ceremony of the Vatican a bore, now suddenly are touched and grief-stricken. The great buildings that line the Square and form the frontier between Italy and Vatican City are hung with white-and-yellow flags at half mast. Priests, nuns, and the devout go trooping slowly by, fingering their rosaries and gazing upward at the windows of the third floor where the Popes reside. Today, as a sign of mourning, the blinds of the private apartment are closed tight.

In the right-hand colonnade, the Door of Bronze is closed, and Swiss Guards in fatigue uniform are patrolling the Vatican's most famous frontier. Beside the portal a big white notice edged with black has been posted on the wall, announcing to the Romans that the Pope is dead.

Night and day, great torches burn about the Pontiff. Motionless, in dress uniforms of red and silver, the Noble Guards stand watch with swords drawn. At their backs, a little farther removed, are drawn up the Swiss Guards with steel cuirasses and plumed helms.

And all this while, before the Papal altar canopied with Bernini's baldachin, offices for the soul's repose of the Head of the Church continue day in, day out. There a lofty catafalque has been erected, ringed about by twenty-four flaming torches and sixty-six candles and surmounted by the Papal tiara.

For three days the devout have filed past the Pope and said their prayers for him. At the end of the third day, the cathedral doors are closed and the Sovereign Pontiff begins the final stage of his long journey toward the tomb. He is carried into another chapel; and there, in the presence of the diplomatic corps, the Roman nobility, high dignitaries of the Church, and close friends, the body, still attired in its pontifical vestments, is wrapped in the great red-silk drapery of the funeral couch, now serving as a shroud. At his feet is placed a purse of red velvet containing an example of every medal and coin struck during his pontificate. Into a metal tube is sealed a parchment listing the memorable achievements of the departed Pope. This testimonial will go with him into the tomb.

The body now is placed in a triple casket, one made of cypress with a lining of red silk, the second of lead, the third of oak. The three caskets receive a last absolution and find temporary sepulture in the crypt of the Basilica of St. Peter.

Popes, as a rule, provide detailed instructions regarding the spot where they wish to be laid away. Guided by feelings of affinity for a certain one of their predecessors, they select a spot not far from his tomb. All, however, are resolved to be buried here on this Vatican Hill where, in the long ago, the first of their long line, Peter, was crucified head downward, and where today his tomb is venerated beneath Michelangelo's vast and luminous dome.

XXXIV

Víva íl Papa!

FOLLOWING THE DEATH OF
the Pope, the Dean of the Sacred College calls a daily
meeting of all cardinals present at Rome. Their first general assembly opens with a reading of the Constitution,
as revised during the pontificate of Pius XII,* in which

* Pius XII's codified revision dates from 1945.

is prescribed, down to the last detail, the order of procedure for the election of a new Pope. At the close of the
reading, every cardinal takes an oath to be bound by the
Constitution.

The cardinals then determine the manner in which
the solemn obsequies shall be conducted during a nine-
day period, and they appoint two ecclesiastics, one to
pronounce the eulogy of the late Pope and the other to
deliver an exhortation to the cardinals who are about to
elect his successor. They also arrange for the reception
of the diplomatic corps and the various knightly orders.
Several committees of the cardinalate are named to desig-
nate all persons to be summoned to assist in preparations
for the Conclave. The cardinals next look into estimates
of the expenses that the Conclave will entail. Letters
received from sovereigns and Chiefs of State now are
read to them, and reports from the nuncios; and they hear
a reading of whatever documents the deceased Pope had
planned to address to the Sacred College.

Then in their presence the Fisherman's ring, engraved
with a representation of St. Peter and worn by the most
recent Sovereign Pontiff, is broken. The seal hitherto used
by the Apostolic Chancellery is likewise shattered. Lots
are drawn for the cells that the cardinals shall respectively
occupy during the Conclave, and the day and hour are
set for it to begin. At the death of Benedict XV, the
interval of delay prescribed by the Constitution was so
short that an American cardinal was not able to arrive
in time to take part in the balloting. Following his election, Pius XI amended that article so as to forbid the
holding of the Conclave until fifteen or eighteen days
after the Pope's death. Now it would seem necessary to
revise that article back again, for transportation has become so swift that cardinals traveling to Rome will run

the risk of finding themselves idle for a few days while waiting for the election to get under way.

As the funeral ceremonies go forward at the Vatican and St. Peter's, the Princes of the Church in distant parts are hastily preparing for their journeys. Pope Pius XII will not be able to witness the results of one of the outstanding reforms of his pontificate. For the first time, the majority of the Papal electors will be non-Italians—nor will the cardinals of the Curia constitute more than a small minority. Representatives of the Churches *in partibus,* including among them Eastern patriarchs, a Chinese cardinal, and a Hindu, will figure among the electors of the Head of the Church.

As more and more cardinals arrive at Rome, they proceed with a sort of straw-vote Conclave. Not being shut up in the Vatican as yet, they make contacts and engage in discreet exchanges of impressions. National affinities and the gravitational pull of certain powers—France, Spain, the United States—come now into play.

In the Eternal City, predictions start building up. Bored though they are by the ceremonial doings of the Vatican, the Romans quickly grow heated over the election. Everybody repeats the old saw, "The Pope who goes into the Conclave comes out a cardinal." By which is meant, of course, that the cardinals who are most obviously "Papal timber" stand the smallest chance of election. As with all popular sayings, this one is by no means infallible. Nobody was a more obvious choice in 1939 than Cardinal Pacelli, yet he was elected. His immediate predecessor, on the other hand, Pius XI, did not even figure to be in the running.

Quite apart from whatever personal prestige and popularity may seem to favor one or another of the Princes of the Church, discussion always boils down to the question of whether it would be more advisable to have a "pastoral" Pope or a "political" one. Some will favor the election of the head of a great diocese who has been trained by seeing life as it is and so can bring to the throne of St. Peter a first-hand experience of human needs. Others, perhaps more closely acquainted with the pitfalls of Roman life, will favor a cardinal, versed in the ways of the Curia, who has come up through the treadmill and thus gained experience in Church government and world affairs. The fact is, however, that like rarely follows like in pontificates. Each finds itself confronted with a different set of circumstances and brings to the Church an individual stamp.

A dense coat of whitewash has been laid over the corridor windows so that nobody from outside can signal to persons in conclave. Hoardings have been erected to close off all entries to the quadrangle formed by the Sistine Chapel and the Vatican apartments where the Conclave is to be held. In the centers of these barriers, "turnabouts" have been constructed, the kind used in the convents of enclosed religious orders. Only by pivoting these turrets about can provisions be passed in to the prisoners. Throughout the Conclave, in short, the cardinals and their assistants will be cut off from the outside world.

Every elector has the right to take in with him two "conclavists," either two clerics or one cleric and one layman. The cardinal who brings them must vouch for the purity of their morals, their powers of discretion, and their love for the Holy See. Locked up during the Conclave, in addition to the cardinals and their assistants, will be the recording secretary of the Sacred College, the chaplain, the prefect of Apostolic ceremonies, a monk to hear confessions, two physicians, a surgeon, a pharmacist with several assistants, and various other service personnel.

Pius XII has lately had a series of rooms furnished to serve as "cells" for the cardinals meeting in Conclave. Every cell is in fact a small flat consisting of a bedroom for the cardinal, a study, and quarters for the conclavists. These lodgings leave something to be desired in the way of comfort, although they do represent a great step forward from the days of Pius XI. The Guardroom of the Borgia Apartments usually is assigned to serve as dining hall for the cardinals, who take their meals together around a table shaped like a horseshoe. Altars are set up in various of the Vatican rooms.

The Sistine Chapel is the traditional polling place. Down the length of the Chapel walls are canopies of green cloth, each surmounting a little platform on which are placed a chair and a small table. And there, side by side, the members of the Sacred College take their places.

Before going into the Chapel, the cardinals gather in St. Peter's and their ranking member celebrates the Mass of the Holy Ghost. The cardinals hear a sermon exhorting them (so runs the Constitution of Pius XII, wherein he has amended and codified the laws of the Conclave) to give to the Holy Roman and Universal Church a capable pastor, and to do so in the shortest possible time and with the greatest zeal, unmindful of all earthly affections and having their regard fixed solely upon God.

"Divine ceremonies being concluded," writes Pius XII, "the Conclave shall be entered into without delay, or not later than that evening, as it may please the Fathers. The Master of Ceremonies shall lead the way with the Papal Cross: he shall be followed by the cardinals, all vested with robes and wearing the mozetta of violet wool, with the silk belt of the same color and with the plain rochet. The crucifer shall be followed by Choristers chanting the hymn, *Veni, Creator Spiritus."*

In the Chapel, more prayers follow. The prefect of Apostolic ceremonies then proclaims: *"Extra omnes!"* That is the signal for all to leave who are not to be shut in with the cardinals. The latter now hear read again the Constitution establishing the rules for the election, and they all solemnly swear to be bound by those. Whereafter they repeat in unison:

"We do promise, declare, and swear that whichever of us, by the will of God, shall be elected Roman Pontiff, he shall never cease to defend and vigorously assert all rights of the Sovereign Pontiff, including the temporal rights and those of his temporal sovereignty as well as the independence of the Holy See. Immediately after his election to the pontificate, he shall swear to be mindful of this pledge.

"We promise and do solemnly swear . . . that we ourselves and our retainers or conclavists will keep secret all that appertains in any way whatsoever to the election of the Roman Pontiff and to all that shall be done in Conclave; we pledge ourselves not to break this secrecy, either during the Conclave or after the election of the new Pope, unless the latter dispenses us so to do. We will not accept in any wise from any power whatsoever, and regardless of whatsoever pretext, the mission of communicating a veto or exclusion by even so much as the merest preference expressed, and we will not make known that veto before the assembly of the Sacred College, nor to a Cardinal privately, whether in writing or by word of mouth, either directly or indirectly, nor by sign or any other means, whether before the Conclave or during the course of it. Moreover, we will support no intervention or intercession of whatsoever sort by which the power of the laity might seek to intervene in the election of the Sovereign Pontiff."

Finally, after one last exhortation from the Dean of the Sacred College, it is the turn of the governor of the Conclave, the perpetual marshal of the Holy Roman Church, the archbishops in attendance at the pontifical threshold (whose duty it will be to supervise the Conclave's "turnabouts"), together with all other attendant prelates, to swear in the presence of all the cardinals that they will, in conformity with the rules prescribed, carry out their duties.

Pius XII lays down certain more detailed instructions, as follows: "The lights shall be turned on, whereafter three Cardinals, the heads of orders, and the Chamberlain, accompanied by the secretary of the Conclave, the prefect and the Apostolic masters of ceremony, together with the architect of the Conclave, shall make a diligent and thorough search to assure themselves that no person or spy lurks in hiding. This tour of inspection having been accomplished, the Conclave is closed and the keys are entrusted to the Cardinal-Chamberlain and the prefect of Apostolic ceremonies. . . ." Whereafter all the conclavists are to be assembled in the Chapel and passed in review one by one.

The Conclave is closed simultaneously from the inside by the Cardinal-Chamberlain and from the outside by the marshal of the Conclave and his assistants. The keys to the outer doors are entrusted to the marshal-warden. Once the double locking-up has been accomplished, an affidavit to that effect is posted inside and outside.

During the term of the Conclave, cardinals especially assigned to the job are to visit the cells of their confrères at frequent intervals, so as to make sure their seclusion has not been violated. The Pope decrees that nothing shall reach the cardinals from without, neither letters nor newspapers and magazines. Nor may the cardinals send out anything; always excepting the Cardinal Grand Penitentiary, who shall continue in touch with his tribunal, since problems of conscience alone can brook of no delay. Excommunication in the severest form will fall upon any persons who introduce photographic, radio, television, or cinematic devices into the Conclave.

Meanwhile, a tailor is hastily cutting out three white cassocks in small, medium, and large, respectively, so that everything will be in readiness for the new Pope. In the sacristy of the Sistine Chapel, servants are giving a little cast-iron stove a trial run. That is where the slips will be burnt after every balloting. If the vote does not yield the prescribed majority, a little damp straw goes into the stove along with the ballot slips so that the black smoke coming out of the chimney may announce to the Roman populace jamming St. Peter's Square that the Pope "has not been made yet." A temporary bedchamber is being readied, too, in the event that the Sovereign Pontiff should be elected that very evening.

The morning after the Conclave goes in, all cardinals except the infirm, who remain in their cells, assemble in the Sistine Chapel and the election begins. Every elector receives two or three blanks on which are printed in Latin:

> *Eligo in Summum Pontificem Rev.mum*
> *D. Meum D. Card . . .*
> ("I choose as Sovereign Pontiff the Most
> Reverend Lord Cardinal . . ."

Upon a table before the fresco of the "Last Judgment" stands a chalice covered with a patten. Every elector, after filling out his blank in a disguised hand so that the tellers may not recognize it, comes in turn before the table. He kneels in prayer, then rises and declares in a loud and clear voice:

"The Lord Christ who shall be my judge is witness that I choose the one whom I believe should be chosen before God."

He then places his ballot on the patten and tips it into the chalice. Whereupon, after reverencing the high altar, he returns to his place. As for cardinals who are ill, three Cardinals-Infirmary make the rounds of their cells, carrying a ballot box.

When everyone has voted, the First Cardinal-Teller stirs the chalice and the Last Cardinal-Teller proceeds with the sorting-out of the ballots. All the electors note down the results of every balloting upon a specially prepared tally sheet.

Up until now, a two-thirds majority has been sufficient to elect a Pope. However, since the reforms of Pius XII, regulations require that the majority be one more than two-thirds of the total, so that it cannot be said that the successful candidate voted for himself, which is illegal.

The Pope urges that the cardinals refuse to commit

themselves to agreements or by pledges or compacts. But
he does authorize the reaching of understandings in favor
of such-and-such a candidate. And lastly, Pius XII addresses a warm appeal to the one who shall be chosen,
exhorting him to accept unhesitatingly the burden thus
laid upon him.

When a majority has been found, every cardinal gives
a tug to the pulley cord that hangs beside his place and
so lowers the little canopy over it. Only the baldachin
of the one newly elected remains open—the first token of
his sovereignty. The ranking cardinal, in the name of the
Sacred College, then asks him whether he accepts his
election and, after receiving that assurance, inquires
under what name he will choose to reign. And then, after
the first doing of homage to the new Pope by the Princes
of the Church, a member of the Sacred College goes out
on to the balcony overlooking St. Peter's Square, where
the immense crowd already knows that a Pope has been
elected—the last plume of smoke from the sacristy stove
having come out white because no wet straw was added.
But the Roman crowd still does not know who is elected.
So then the cardinal shouts the joyous proclamation,
which no doubt, after the next Conclave that is held,
will be sent echoing by loud speakers clear to the banks
of the Tiber:

"Nuntio vobis gaudium magnum: Habemus Papam!"
("I announce to you tidings of great joy! We have a
Pope, the Most Reverend Lord Cardinal . . .")

Several days later the new Pope will make his entry
into St. Peter's. He follows the same progression as the

dead Pontiff, from the Sistine Chapel to the Chapel of the Holy Sacrament to the tomb of the Apostle. He is carried, seated upon his throne, framed by the *flabelli*, enormous fans which have descended to the Papal Court by somewhat indirect inheritance from the Pharaohs. And now once again the basilica is a burst of lights and acclamations. The silver trumpets blast their hymns toward the living statue that pivots to right and left in benediction. The Sistine choristers sing motets as clouds of incense, shot through with the rays of morning, mount toward the dome.

The Papal cortege moves onward amid an extraordinary medley of chants and cheering, invocations, lights, and aromatics. Before the throne of the Pope, where he sways aloft above the crowd, walks a master of ceremonies. He is carrying a long silver baton to the tip of which he has tied a wad of smoldering hemp, which gives off a thin and acrid smoke. And every so often, addressing the Pope, he says to him: "Most Holy Father, so passes away the glory of the world."

A few hours more, and the new Pope will become acquainted with that glory when, on the balcony of the basilica, he is crowned with the tiara before the crowd of assembled Romans: the tiara, that triple crown which once encircled the brows of the Kings of Persia and is never worn by the Pope in purely religious ceremonials.

What is more, the Coronation, a spectacular ceremony which takes place before the delegations sent by all the nations of the earth and the horde of pilgrims overflowing from St. Peter's Square all up and down the banks of the Tiber, adds nothing to the Papal dignity. The Pope is Head of the Church from the moment when, in the cloistered silence of the Sistine Chapel, he accepts his

election at the hands of those who were his peers in the
Sacred College. As of that instant, he possesses the full
powers of the pontificate. All the rest is secondary.

There is not a gesture, not a word, however, in the interminable and gaudy pageantry by which the Pope is
conducted to the tomb of St. Peter and from there out
to the view of the crowd—symbols themselves, and representatives of the whole world—which does not have
profound significance, going back, as all of it does, to
the very fountainheads of power, both sacred and profane.

A red banner ornamented with the pontifical crossed
keys has been hung from the loggia, a nacelle jutting out
upon the façade of the basilica, high above the heads of
the crowd. Curious and enthralled, bishops by the dozen
are leaning their mitered heads over the balustrade to
get a better view of the Romans as they clamor for the
new Pontiff.

At last he makes his appearance. After the exhausting
rites in the basilica, he has snatched a few moments' rest
in a small room fitted up behind the loggia for the occasion. Palms pressed together, he stands ready and waiting.
A Cardinal-Deacon turns and faces him. There between
them, on a red cushion, is the tiara, sparkling with bril-
liants. Earlier, borne along on its velvet bed in the processional, it already has played a mute but garish part in the
festivities. Slowly the cardinal lifts it and places it on the
head of the Pope, who straightens up and faces toward
the crowd. And then, spreading wide his arms, he gives
his first benediction *urbi et orbi.*

XXXV

The Soul of the Church

FROM THE OUTSET, MY object has been to explore not the Church itself but the Vatican. I have focused my newspaperman's curiosity upon the chief agencies of Church government and the "big wheels," so to speak, that keep the machinery of administration turning: the Curia and the Congregations, the cardinals and the State Secretariat. It has been my endeavor, also, to discover toward what far horizons the barque of Peter the Fisherman is gradually shifting its course; what new lands are opening before his missionaries; to what fresh tasks the laymen will be called. But the Church, to use that word in its fullest meaning, is still more than all that.

As propounded by theologians, the Church is the mystical body of Christ, who is, in the belief of the devout, the Son of God. Consequently—and here the subject eludes all mundane "reportage"—the Church, sharing with Christ his dual nature, is at once both human and divine. Were the Church to lose this divine embodiment, this intimate union with God which is compared by theologians to the union of man and wife, it would crumble to dust and the whole structure we have explored in the foregoing chapters would, being mortal, perish. It is comparable to a body which lives only so long as it is inhabited by a soul. And this life-giving power is known to theologians as Divine Grace.

But, even though these instrumentalities would without Grace be dead, the purpose they serve is nonetheless essential. The Church hierarchy—Pope and bishops, pastors and their flocks—is inherent in the Church's very nature. It would be inconceivable without them. In short, the Church is a visible association, made for man. Its founder is Jesus Christ, who has come to redeem mankind from Original Sin through his suffering and death. His legacy, the New Testament and the Sacraments, he bequeaths to his disciples, whom he personally forms into an association at once human and divine, which is the Church. He calls men to be his Apostles, and one of these he singles out to be the particular guardian of his legacy. In their turn, setting the pattern as bishops, the disciples, by the laying on of hands, ordain priests for the administration of the Sacraments. And around these gather the community of the devout, who thus are bonded fast to the life of the primitive Church. Despite all its ramifications, the Church of the Atomic Era, beneath the sometimes suffocating overgrowth, is constructed about those same essential elements: Pope, bishops, priests, and people.

The men who make up the cadre of the Church hierarchy are therefore administrators of a legacy. That legacy in nowise depends upon their individual merit but is a treasure which they can not debase in the dispensing, regardless of how unworthy they may be. Being men, the men of the Church are liable to every human frailty. The priest who consecrates the wafer may be a whoremonger or a murderer—and the sacrifice he performs will add sacrilege to the number of his sins. But the consecration will be valid, the Sacrament efficacious at the behest of a man who has been duly chosen and ordained; for the man is naught, the priestly function all. The Pope may be a Borgia—but, albeit unworthily, he is nonetheless the visible Head of the Church. And apologists, drawing from this an argument in support of the Church's vitality, point out that never a one of the unworthiest of the Popes has availed himself of his power to vitiate the Church's doctrinal and sacramental legacy or impair the repository of the Faith in the slightest degree.

So, then, the life of the Church may be said to be unfolding, at one and the same time, upon two levels, the human plane and the plane of Divine Grace. But, without the other, neither would be able to exist, just as

man would not exist as only body or only soul. Furthermore, the Church will be found most flourishing wherever
Grace abounds in fullest measure, and least vigorous
where the structure built by men is not endued with
Grace. Wherefore it often happens that the Church is to
be seen at its most resplendent in some abode where
there is true sanctity, perhaps in a country parish or a
hovel in the slums and not beneath the canopy of a
cardinal. The Church, therefore, when viewed in the
largest sense, is the sum of all its members, who are of
course linked to Head and hierarchy, but are for their
own part suffused with a vitality as effectual and necessary to the whole as are the bishops and the priests.

Nor is this all. For the Church, going yet further, proclaims that by virtue of its dual nature it extends beyond
the confines of mortality. Its mystical body lives also
beyond the grave. The living and the dead—who, for the
Church, are even more truly living—are united in a single,
an organic, entity, and are in a sense accountable to one
another. Here we have what theologians call the Communion of Saints. And this dogma teaches that every
man shares in the community of life, that all have life
through one another: all men being sharers in the common treasure, which every man either adds to or depletes.

The Communion of Saints thus comprises, in the eyes
of the Church, all those who enrich the life of Grace. But
is this merely one way of saying that such "communion"
is limited to the minority of mankind who make up the
Church of Rome, and that all others are excluded?

By no means. And this is so because the domain of
Grace is the domain of freedom. Grace, according to
God's will, may be visited upon whomsoever it chooses,
nor does it refuse those who seek it if their search is

earnest and profound. Like a sun which lightens all those, no matter how far off, who open their eyes to see, or who, even though unconsciously and as if by instinct are impelled to seek its warmth, Grace is ready to shed the divine influence upon all "men of good will." And so, according to the Church's doctrine, all men whatsoever may share in the life of the Church's soul, whether they be Catholics, Orthodox, Protestants, Jews, Mohammedans, or those who are claimed by no denomination. Their membership in the soul of the Church is their personal affair, their own soul's secret, and their participation in the treasure shared by the Communion of Saints will be made known only upon that day when the Last Judgment proceeds to the final reassessment of all values.

It is Divine Grace which gives not only life but freedom, and Grace is operative through the Sacraments instituted by Christ. Of these, the greatest is the Eucharist. For the veritable Incarnation of Christ is endlessly repeated in the Sacrament of the Altar; and thus, through the Mass, the supernatural character of the Church is continually renewed. Moreover, by Grace is every man transformed, or, as the theologians say, "sanctified": he being thereby raised from the human level to that of the Divine. His membership in the Church then ceases to have the nature of constraint. He is at one with the Church in the spirit of love. The realm of Grace is the realm of Charity.

So now it may be seen how dogma is no theoretical assertion of truth imposed under penalty of sanction, but is instead a shared experience of truth revealed. The hierarchical structure becomes no longer a "system of constraints" but an integral scale of ascent toward the summit. And that summit, comprehending the realms of Freedom, Charity, and Grace, is Christ Himself, the founder of the Church. Thus, in the eyes of Catholics, although the organization of the Church is confided to the faltering powers of men, the Church itself is continually transfigured and revived by Him who stands as purpose and impulsion of its ageless journey, the beginning and the end.

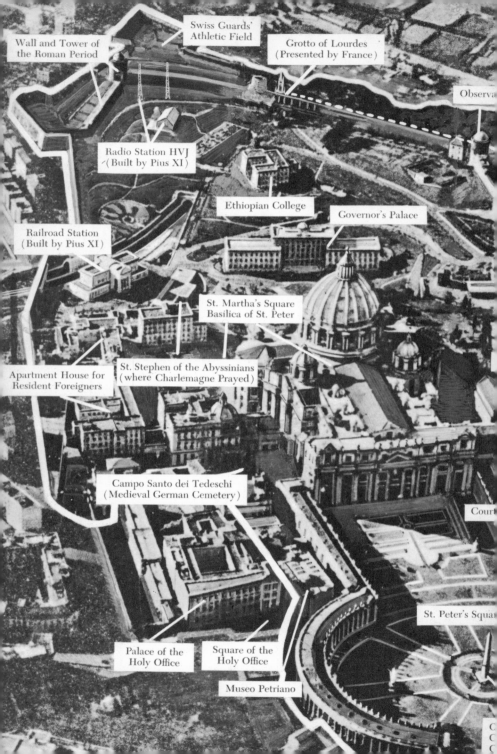

Wall and Tower of
the Roman Period

Swiss Guards'
Athletic Field

Grotto of Lourdes
(Presented by France)

Observa

Radio Station HVJ
(Built by Pius XI)

Ethiopian College

Governor's Palace

Railroad Station
(Built by Pius XI)

St. Martha's Square
Basilica of St. Peter

Apartment House for
Resident Foreigners

St. Stephen of the Abyssinians
(where Charlemagne Prayed)

Campo Santo dei Tedeschi
(Medieval German Cemetery)

Court

St. Peter's Squar

Palace of the
Holy Office

Square of the
Holy Office

Museo Petriano